Praise fo

M000078460

"Attunement *is a beautiful guide into the subtle and loving realms of Spirit. With refreshing transparency about her own challenging journey to deep spiritual awakening, Marisa opens the door for even the most cautious among us to successfully experience the support and reassurance of our beloved helpers on the other side. A wonderful book."*
— **Sonia Choquette**, New York Times best-selling author of
The Answer Is Simple and *Waking Up in Paris*

"*Exciting, powerful, and remarkably easy meditation techniques for taking control of your inner journey, and thereby stepping up the adventure of your life*"
— **Mike Dooley**, New York Times best-selling author of
Infinite Possibilities and *Playing the Matrix*

"*Get ready to do some deep spiritual exploration. This book is packed with excellent exercises to discover the truth of your soul! You'll discover ways of looking at life that perhaps you've never explored before.*"
— **Denise Linn**, best-selling author of
Soul Coaching and *Energy Strands*

"*In* Attunement, *Marisa Moris offers a unique guide to the energies that are available to every human being for self-healing. The exercises in this book will help you connect to these energies, and will benefit you and those you love.*"
— **Dr. Ervin Laszlo**, Nobel Prize nominee,
author of *Science and the Akashic Field*

"*Clearly written and creatively expressed,* Attunement *provides a beautiful home for inspiring personal understanding and spiritual evolution.*"
— **Gary E. Schwartz**, Ph.D., professor, The University of
Arizona, and author of *The Energy Healing Experiments,
The Sacred Promise,* and *Super Synchronicity*

ATTUNEMENT

Hay House Titles of Related Interest

YOU CAN HEAL YOUR LIFE, the movie,
starring Louise Hay & Friends
(available as a 1-DVD program, an expanded 2-DVD set,
and an online streaming video)
Learn more at www.hayhouse.com/louise-movie

THE SHIFT, the movie,
starring Dr. Wayne W. Dyer
(available as a 1-DVD program, an expanded 2-DVD set,
and an online streaming video)
Learn more at www.hayhouse.com/the-shift-movie

***

*THE CHOICE FOR LOVE: Entering into a New, Enlightened
Relationship with Yourself, Others & the World,*
by Dr. Barbara De Angelis

*CORE LIGHT HEALING: My Personal Journey and Advanced
Healing Concepts for Creating the Life You Long to Live,*
by Barbara Ann Brennan

*EVERYTHING IS HERE TO HELP YOU:
A Guide to Your Soul's Evolution,* by Matt Kahn

*WISDOM FROM YOUR SPIRIT GUIDES: A Handbook to Contact
Your Soul's Greatest Teachers,* by James Van Praagh

*YOUR 3 BEST SUPER POWERS: Meditation,
Imagination & Intuition,* by Sonia Choquette

All of the above are available at your local bookstore,
or may be ordered by visiting:

Hay House USA: www.hayhouse.com®
Hay House Australia: www.hayhouse.com.au
Hay House UK: www.hayhouse.co.uk
Hay House India: www.hayhouse.co.in

ATTUNEMENT

Align with Your Source, Become Your Creator Self, and Manifest a Life You Love

MARISA MORIS

HAY HOUSE, INC.
Carlsbad, California • New York City
London • Sydney • New Delhi

Published in the United States by: Hay House, Inc.: www.hayhouse
.com® • **Published in Australia by:** Hay House Australia Pty. Ltd.: www
.hayhouse.com.au • **Published in the United Kingdom by:** Hay House
UK, Ltd.: www.hayhouse.co.uk • **Published in India by:** Hay House Publishers India: www.hayhouse.co.in

Cover design: Barbara LeVan Fisher
Interior design: Karim J. Garcia

Library of Congress Cataloging-in-Publication Data

Names: Moris, Marisa, author.
Title: Attunement : align with your source, become your creator self,
and
    manifest a life you love / Marisa Moris.
Description: 1st Edition. | Carlsbad : Hay House, Inc., 2018.
Identifiers: LCCN 2018016397 | ISBN 9781401954918 (tradepaper : alk.
paper)
Subjects: LCSH: Spiritual life--Miscellanea. | Guides (Spiritualism) |
    Spiritualism.
Classification: LCC BL624 .M6664 2018 | DDC 133.9--dc23 LC record
available at https://lccn.loc.gov/2018016397

Tradepaper ISBN: 978-1-4019-5491-8
e-book ISBN: 978-1-4019-5492-5

10 9 8 7 6 5 4 3 2 1
1st edition, July 2018

Printed in the United States of America

Certified Chain of Custody
SUSTAINABLE   Promoting Sustainable Forestry
FORESTRY
INITIATIVE   www.sfiprogram.org
SFI-01268

SFI label applies to text stock

CONTENTS

"Always be humble and gentle.

Be patient with each other,

making allowance for each other's
faults because of your love.

Make every effort to keep yourselves
united in the Spirit,

binding yourselves together with peace."

—Ephesians 4:2-3

INTRODUCTION

Growing up in a Christian household, I had a working knowledge of the Bible and the idea of God, but what I learned never quite resonated like it was supposed to. It wasn't until my spiritual awakening that my thirst for knowledge of this Almighty Being surfaced.

I was not born with the ability to see, hear, or talk to spirits. I didn't know I had the ability to see or heal the future. I didn't realize I could feel the emotions or hear the thoughts of others around me. And I certainly did not know I could channel the consciousness of anyone or anything, let alone an angel or a guide. And because I was unaware of these gifts, they became more a curse than a blessing.

By the time I was 15 years old, I had so many thoughts, feelings, and desires that belonged to others swarming around my head 24/7 that I didn't know what to do, and I began misinterpreting them. It got so bad that these foreign energies manifested as self-hate, changing me almost overnight. I went from being a confident, caring, loving overachiever to a resentful, angry, vengeful, and almost evil young woman. I hated everything and everyone. I abandoned my childhood friends and got kicked off the varsity softball team, my grades dropped, and I took up smoking. Now, looking back, it is clear to me that when I was 15, I picked up a spirit attachment, which was causing my self-destructive behavior.

Unfortunately, I didn't know anything about spirits or attachment at the time, and when I turned 18, my self-destructive behavior got even worse. I turned to drugs and an unhealthy, co-dependent relationship. I focused all my attention on enabling and trying to fix a boyfriend who would never love me back. And the drugs shielded me from all those feelings I had no way of processing but had begun experiencing years before. (They weren't my feelings, so how could I know how to process them?) And because of this, my life became one of plotting how I would get my next fix. Thankfully, years later, I was able to pull out of this spiral, but not without experiencing some very real tragedies.

Even though I finally managed to put my life back together, I still didn't know what to do with the feelings and thoughts that bombarded me. But then, in May 2008, at the age of 30, I met my first guide.

I had just bought a brand-new Mercedes and was coming home in a rush because I was late meeting my dad for church. I got off the freeway, made a left turn, and began heading toward the hill that would take me home.

The next thing I saw was completely unbelievable. I was standing above an accident scene with a girl who looked like me, only she was about two feet taller. She had green eyes and blonde hair. On my left was a huge ball of light. As if I had known her forever, I began talking to her. I said in frustration, "There is *no* way I am going back. Marisa is an idiot. Look at her! She crashed her car, she's going to lose her license, and she has no clue how broke and unhappy she is about to be! I am *not* doing it anymore, and you can't make me!"

The tall girl just looked at me with true unconditional love in her eyes. She laid her hand on my right shoulder, and instantly I was light, I was all-knowing. I knew who I was and why I was on earth. She said, "You have to go back; there are too many people to help."

My response to that was, "Help people do what? No thank you." I began to walk away, though I was still feeling like I had never felt before. I still can't describe it to this day, but it was heavenly.

Next thing I knew, I woke up soaking wet, with medics and police officers surrounding me. I had blacked out, had a seizure, hit a fire hydrant, and apparently almost drowned in my own car.

My life following the accident was a living hell. I thought I had hit bottom in the years when I struggled with drugs, but that wasn't even close. I couldn't remember anything for longer than a day or two, so my business suffered. I had to move in with my dad, and I was stripped of my driver's license and therefore my independence. I needed to be with someone 24 hours a day just in case I had another episode. And over the next few months, I had a seizure about every two weeks; sometimes three weeks if I was lucky.

Although when I had those seizures I never saw the girl who looked like me, I would still regain the feeling I'd had when I was out of my body that night. It was the feeling of not being tied to this earth, of knowing who I was, where I was going, and what my purpose was. When I was out of my body, I didn't hurt. The feeling was true bliss. After what seemed to be a lifetime, I would abruptly come right back to my body, and I would be told I had only been unconscious for a few minutes. And when that happened, I felt nothing but pain and sadness. I didn't want to be in my body. I wanted to leave again.

I did eventually get my license back, but less than a year later, I got in *another* accident. I wasn't hurt that time (and I *had* been taking my seizure medications), but I had another out-of-body experience, and I saw the tall blonde girl again.

I was so angry with her. She had sent me back, she hadn't said good-bye, and she had left me completely alone!

She said, "We have been with you. We've been here the whole time. You just can't hear us through Marisa's mind."

This triggered my anger even more. I yelled at them about how frustrating Marisa was. I told them, "I can't handle it! Not only does she not hear you, she won't listen to me at all!" The tall girl just smiled at me and placed her hand on my right shoulder, and—*bam!*—I woke up in the local emergency room with my dad next to me, scared out of his mind.

It was a long road from there to here, but since then I've received and delivered messages from a countless number of dimensions and planes. The beings sending messages through from "above" range from soul family members on the other side, to passed family members, to ascended masters like Saint Germaine or Mary Magdalene and Archangels. And I have come to understand that "the guides" are all different layers of my connection to Source.

There's a belief that God said, "Let there be light beings that can carry my essence," and then there were souls. That piece of us all that is a tiny bit of God—it is in

4

you too. Would you believe me if I told you that *you* are that beacon of light God summoned? Would you believe me if I told you that *you* are God?

As crazy as it may sound, through my years and years of channeling with the guides, this is the greatest knowledge I've come to embrace. We are all a piece of God Consciousness experiencing life through our own creations, learning lessons we long ago assigned our pieces of self, and fulfilling carefully planned-out missions. We just have a case of soul amnesia!

It's time to say good-bye to that so-called soul amnesia. Because I am here to help you remember who you are, why you are here, and how to fully connect with that original energy or divine spark, that broke off from Source. I am so excited that this book has found its way into your hands, because it means you are ready to change your life *now*!

I am going to teach some of what I have learned about creation, and I'm going to do it in the most fun way possible: I am going to reconnect you to your divine spark, your spirit, and all the different layers of your multidimensional soul—from your human body to that piece of God in you. I am going to teach you to use intention, commands, and your imagination to embody your divinity, which will allow you to meet and become your Creator Self. And once you meet this all-powerful version of yourself, the self that lives outside of this reality, the self that created your life . . . you will be able to consciously become the creator that you have always unconsciously been . . .

HOW TO USE
THIS BOOK

Do you remember hearing that in 2012, according to the Mayan calendar, the "end of the world" was upon us? Well, according to my guides, really it was just the end of the world as we knew it. In 2008 there was a shift in consciousness that created a shift in energy; human beings began to see life differently. No matter how closed-minded or how logical or unemotional the human mind was, by 2012 we would all be forced into a reality where we would not be able to *help* but wonder if there was something more to life.

This is why since 2012 there are so many people seeking knowledge about Spirit, working on the emotional issues they have shoved away for so long. There are people like me, who have gone from having completely "normal," nonspiritual, unemotional lives to being full-blown self-help and spirituality addicts.

This shift can be scary—partly because society as a whole is not aware of it. We ought to be celebrating how we are elevating our consciousness, but instead we are at war, with people killing other people over who they believe God is. As we gain access to higher levels of spirituality, we can also misinterpret our own experience, believing we or those we love have autism, sexual dysmorphia, depression, bipolar disorder, and so on and so forth. Since "the end of the world as we knew it" in December 2012, my guides have told me that everyone on the planet is now empathic. This, as I know from experience, is a hard burden to bear. Now we have to manage not only our own unruly emotions, but everyone else's as well—so we need to be educated. I know that my empathic abilities were the root of my substance abuse issues; I self-medicated to avoid the overwhelming emotions—emotions I could not possibly process—and I see this happening again and again in people around me.

The Soul House is a metaphor the guides have recently introduced me to. It's a way to understand the different levels of consciousness and layers of self, leading up to your Creator Self and beyond. In this book I am going to take you through the Soul House room by room, each one building upon the next, in order to make you the creator you were always meant to be.

Before we go any further, let me give you a visual. Imagine your consciousness as a little ball of energy. This energy moves up and down a tube of light around your spine. That tube of light goes all the way down into the center of the earth and all the way up to the Source of your creation, your Creator Self. In the middle of this tube, there is also a brilliant silver line. This line is fascinating in that it is actually a loop. The line starts in the middle of Source, in the zero point, travels down through your head, down the center of the spine, into the earth and through it, and then loops back up to Source. I see this as Source's way of experiencing all its creations as well as a way of distributing information through all the layers of you. This is something I call the zero light line, and every day I learn more about this amazing tool the guides have given us. We'll explain this more later on in the book.

The Soul House resides energetically as a golden sphere inside the pineal gland, behind the third eye, in the center of the brain. In order to get there, imagine that little ball of consciousness that you are riding up the zero light line through the tube of light. The guides have used the visual of a glass elevator to make it easy for us to move up and down through our physical bodies with our awareness in the ball of consciousness. To me this elevator looks like the ones you find in an Embassy Suites hotel—you know, where the elevator, with mirrors inside the doors, rises up the center of the lobby, and you look out through the curved glass? The higher you go, the more you can see. The cable it rides, the force pulling it up, is like the zero light line, and the elevator shaft is like the tube of light shining down from the Creator Self. The zero light line is not a being—it is best described as a feedback loop of information and electricity. The tube of light is *yours* and only yours. It is your soul's essence, and as you become more and more used to pulling all your awareness into it, your life mission, your soul plan, and your destiny as a soul living on earth become more and more clear. I am not sure how it happens; it just does. I have seen it happen to students, clients, and myself for the last six years. I am so excited for you to experience it!

Let's try it now. Begin by saying, "I am now in (your name)'s glass elevator," and visualize yourself in it. Imagine what it looks like. It does not need to look like mine—we all have different physical bodies, and this is a representation of your true soul's anatomy, so it's only natural that our energetic bodies, while all having the same parts, will be a little different too. After imagining that you are in the glass elevator, say, "Zero," and bring your awareness to the center of your chest, where you will find a silver ball of light. From it a line shoots through the roof of the elevator, going all the way up to the zero point in Source, and also shoots through the floor of the elevator and out through the center of the earth. Now say in your head, "I am now aligned with my tube of light," and picture a brilliant tube of light from above that shoots down through your elevator. The light is bright and loving. It is the light from your Creator Self, who resides at the top of the Soul House in the Creation Room that you will be attuned to after we have journeyed through all the rooms. Pull all your attention and energy into the tube of light and then say, "I now ask my Creator Self to take me to the Soul House."

Immediately the elevator begins to go up and up, until it is in the center of your head. The doors open, and in front of you there is a long hallway or open space with doors on each side. These doors are numbered one through six. At the very far end of the space, up a set of stairs, is Room Seven. This is your control-panel room, where you can witness life through the eyes of your Creator Self—and any other layer of yourself, or even another person for that matter. You can do a lot of other really cool stuff too, once you are introduced to this room and how to use it.

That final room, which I cannot wait to introduce you to, is the Creation Room. As I mentioned, your Soul House is located in a golden sphere in your head, behind your third eye. The Creation Room is in essence the golden sphere of light in your Creator Self's head. All I know about this space is that when I am able to center myself in it, miracles happen. In that space I *become* my Creator Self.

It is that self who resides outside this reality, on the soul plane, and it is that self who, using the I Am command I will teach you, can change your human existence into something you have only dreamed of! This is so exciting! But before I get too far ahead, let me introduce you to the layers of your soul, or as the guides have referred to them, the rooms in your Soul House.

These are the seven rooms of the Soul House:

1. The Physical Room
2. The Emotional Room
3. The Mental Body Room
4. The Astral Room
5. The God Room
6. The Matrix Room
7. The Creation Room

By learning about each of these rooms, you will begin to understand the big picture of yourself as a creator being—someone who stands outside your Soul House, having created everything in it, only to take a piece of itself to live inside without the knowledge that it is the one who created the house. You are that piece that your Creator Self chipped off of itself. And just like the drop of water from the ocean is still ocean water, you are still the creator. So with that understanding, and with the exercises and attunements I have laid out for you in this book, you will start to be able to live your life to the fullest by manifesting the joy, peace, and happiness you've been searching for. When you are done with this book, you will have the ability to switch between the observer outside the Soul House and the human creation inside the house. It is seriously awesome, and you are going to love it!

The first three rooms of the Soul House are made up of the physical body, the emotions, and the mental body, not to be confused with the intellectual mind only. It is also our divine mind where our intuition comes through and is what most refer to as the Higher Self. Most humans can live their entire lives mainly within the first three rooms—though many of us try to skip over the second room entirely. From a very young age, we are told not to cry—that crying is weak—so we learn to cancel out our emotions, removing ourselves from the sad emotional room into the know-it-all mental body room.

The fourth room is where most spiritually awakened newbies gravitate. These first four rooms combined make up our lives on planet Earth, and together they are what is considered a four-dimensional (4D) reality. Room Four allows you to believe that the human life is a mere illusion, that we are all just spirits living in a human vehicle. It's a place where we can start seeing, feeling, and communicating with spirits. This is the room that no one even knows is in the house until someone we love dies and we go searching the house for that room, to see if it really exists.

Room Five brings us into the fifth dimension. We can go past the confines of earth and earthbound spirits and we can start understanding energy and the soul. This is where our connection to our own individual aspect of Source Energy resides. Remember, this is the piece of you that broke off from the original source as God to come down to earth and live this life. Many religions call this room heaven—it has our created concepts of God and Divinity that we have come up with to define our idea of creation, like the Trinity of the Father, Son, and Holy

Spirit. This room is still just a created version of God, and therefore your soul living in Room Five is not perfect.

To find *pure* truth, we must journey to the Matrix Room, the sixth room. This is where we start to see pure energy, pure frequency, pure sound, pure color . . . as I'm sure you can tell, the key word here is *pure*. In the Matrix Room, there is no projection and there is no misconstruing anything. I see it as a grid that gets programmed into our consciousness, surrounded by an awareness bubble. The silver light of the zero light line (this is the cable our glass elevator rides to arrive at the house) comes from that room. In order to reprogram the subconscious and the other layers of the mind, I call upon the pure essence of particular emotions or ask to experience frequencies like love or joy in pure form in this room.

When you leave the ever-pure sixth room, you will enter the seventh room, which really isn't a room at all. It is more like a waiting area, an observation deck where you can perceive life through the eyes or anyone or anything that your Creator Self has created. This is your Creation Room. Here is where you are creating this life you're living, and it is where you can access Source most directly. Think of Source as the energy from all the rooms of your house, what your layers of self need to pull from and live. Think of it as the sun shining down on your Soul House and illuminating it all.

I mentioned that that we are all experiencing a shift of consciousness. Our planet has been 3D—we have been living in the first three rooms. But since 2012 we are now living on a 4D planet; we have all added living in the fourth room—and many of us, with intention, can move beyond.

I personally was "woken up" to the fourth room when my ex-boyfriend died of a drug overdose. When that happened I was first forced into my second and third rooms to deal with the horrible emotions and memories I had hidden away. And then when I couldn't handle the guilt of honestly believing I had killed him because I had been his enabler for so long, I was forced into the fourth room for some relief from the pain of that trauma. Since then I have moved into the subsequent rooms, suffering the consequences and experiencing the joy of each—as you will too.

Once you get to know each of the seven rooms that make up your own personal Soul House, you will learn how to incorporate them into your daily life in a way that helps you stay connected. This connection will enable you to call upon your Creator Self whenever you need to. I don't want you to just get to know all your layers; I want you to be able to *embody* them at will, to use them to perfect all these extrasensory gifts you are now being opened to. *This* is how you're going to be able to start changing your life in ways you never even imagined possible.

In grounding your consciousness into your Creator Self, aligning that zero light line down your spine and connecting with the heavens and the earth, you give yourself more control over your consciousness. You will no longer beat yourself up for your outbursts or get thrown into a depression you don't understand—because you will no longer get yanked around your different levels. *You* will be able to choose which level you want to inhabit at any given moment. The Soul House serves as a guide for starting to understand all our layers, which in reality are very fluid and sometimes even cross over into one another.

Terms as I Use Them

There are many common phrases that are used throughout the spiritual community, and many of us use them in slightly different ways. Here's what I mean by them:

The Creator Self. After each piece of God breaks off from itself, it becomes an *aware* piece of God. The Creator Self is the awareness that is Source; it knows we are technically all the same, all a part of God, but that we are all experiencing a different reality. This is something that is often called the higher self, but I prefer Creator Self.

The Guides. This is a general term I use for my Creator Self and the crew of spirit workers that watch over me on all dimensions throughout time. For the most part, when I say "the guides," I mean it in the same way you would hear other mediums refer to "Spirit."

Exercises and Attunements

In each section of this book, I'm going to take you through a series of stories, exercises, and attunements, as well as real-life applications that will help you work through anything blocking your ability to reach the next room and beyond. I hope to ease you into your spiritual journey with a little bit of fun—because if we can't laugh at ourselves, then who can we laugh at? Spirituality is fun, I promise you.

The exercises I will be teaching you are solutions to issues you may not even know exist, but once you are made aware of them, I hope you will see that issues you thought were physical or mental are in fact energetic and spiritual. You are a very powerful person—we all are—and if this book found you, then some inner aspect of you needed to remind you of your power and bring you the tools to really start living a life you love!

The attunements in this book will fine-tune your energy system, the way someone would tune a CB radio so that it can clearly receive the frequencies or stations the owner of the radio would like to communicate with. Your human body and aura, just like that radio, will be cleared of things keeping you from hearing what you want to hear. When you are attuned to the stations that put you directly in touch with your guides, angels, and all the layers of your soul, it is harder for interference to come through—interference like unwanted beings, tricksters pretending to be someone they are not, or even fragments of yourself, like your inner child, who might not be very happy at all. With attunement you will get to know the voices and the feeling of the frequencies that are here to help guide you and lead you. You will know when your radio has been thrown off and an imposter or unhelpful frequencies are coming through as well. These attunements will not ensure that you will only be hearing from the best of the best—that is up to your discernment, your faith, and your trust in yourself. But these attunements will help you become a fully aligned and connected vehicle that can carry the light and knowledge needed to complete your soul's mission. It will connect you to the divine, loving piece of yourself, the part of you that wants to roll the windows down in the car and sing at the top of your lungs, not caring what anyone thinks, because it's fun and it feels good!

There is a difference between attunements and exercises, though it might not seem so at first. When I use the word *attunement*, I'm talking about one-time exercises that will permanently set you up to connect with a greater aspect of yourself, similar to a preset on a car radio to a certain station. Just because you are attuned and the station is on a preset button, that does not mean you have to listen to it all the time, but you can if you want. An *exercise*, on the other hand, is a step-by-step practice that is meant to be repeated to maintain the ability to push the preset button and stay connected to the high-frequency energies you have now attuned to. The exercises also have intentions, such as healing, communication with guides, or looking into your own future. Doing attunements more than once is not necessary—but all the attunements can be used as repeated exercises if you enjoy them. I personally use them all as exercises regularly, which is why I have put them in the book; they are my favorites.

Attunement (n.)

attunement: n. a bringing into harmony, 1820, from attune + ment (Online Etymology Dictionary)
attunement: n. being or bringing into harmony; a feeling of being "at one" with another being (Dictionary.com)

Remember, the planet has shifted; we are all empaths, which means we are also all mediums, intuitives, channelers, psychics, clairvoyants, etc. So, what will you do with your newfound spiritual gifts? Will you develop them? Or will you attempt to turn them off and continue life as if they are not there at all? Will you explain their symptoms away, or just avoid them with antidepressants, mood stabilizers, and other mind-altering substances?

As an adult it is your freewill choice to do what you feel is best. But my advice? Hang on to your hat, because you have no idea how amazing life is about to get, *if* you allow it!

Through this book you will be able to answer questions that may have plagued you your entire life. You will learn how to apply your new energy to daily tasks. You may even be able to change that horrible commute you can't stand by manifesting a better job, closer to home! The possibilities are endless, as this attunement to the Soul House is not just some crazy, out-of-the-box spiritual awakening; it's actually a manual to practical living if you choose to make it so.

We will set up practices to help you stay grounded *and* connected to Source. This will ensure that all you've worked on is for your highest and best good. The guides and my Higher Self have infused energies into everything you're going to do in this book; strong and powerful white light energies, and we need to make sure you stay connected so that you are manifesting your true life's purpose.

Once you can begin to align with Source and embody your Creator Self, you will see that this reality you have lived in blindly for so long no longer seems so tough. The things you want will magically appear. The things you couldn't get rid of seem to just disappear. *You* have become the creator of your own reality and it's absolutely amazing. It's impossible to put into words the depth of it. Yes, it's great to feel like we are awakened and spiritual, but it's even better to be able to live a whole day without getting angry at someone who intentionally cuts us off on the freeway. It's even better to set a goal to make five times the amount of money we are making now—and *achieve* it. It's amazing to find true love, lose or gain that weight, or get pregnant with that baby even though we were deemed infertile for over 10 years. *All* of this is possible.

I am so excited to get started on this life-changing spiritual journey with you. I cannot wait for you to have the ability to live your life exactly as you've always wanted—and make your dreams come true!

The Path to the Soul House

When my guides first taught me about the Soul House, I had so many aha moments throughout each day that I started a file on my phone to save all my voice notes and text messages to self. I would be driving and all of a sudden it would hit me that the whole reason for something I experienced was because my perception of reality shifted from one room to another. It was overwhelming!

If I could give my younger self advice about my coming spiritual journey, I would say journal, journal, journal, and then journal some more! Write it all down, send text messages to yourself, make voice notes, or even start a private blog or video blog that you can post your thoughts and experiences on. Trust me, you will thank me for this, because you *will* forget the aha moments. I don't care how amazing an experience you have, you will not remember it in the way you think you would. Do yourself a favor and write it down. You will love reading over your experiences later on; it's so much fun!

Exercise: Automatic Writing

Part of journaling is getting clear about what exactly you want to be focusing on. The following exercise requires no experience with meditation or energy or spirits or anything like that, but it tunes you in to something called your genius—the best version of your mind.

Sit down in a place where you can have five minutes to yourself.

Take a few deep breaths in through your nose and out through your mouth while bringing all your awareness into the center of your chest.

Say, "I am now my genius."

From above you, a bright silver, white, or platinum orb of light appears and begins to drop down into your head.

When it is in your head, bring your awareness into it and then continue to breathe. As you breathe the sphere gets bigger and bigger until it's the size of a helmet around your head.

Say, "I ask that my subconscious mind connect with my genius and that my ego and my intellect step aside now."

Write a question to your genius, and then just start writing the answer. Don't judge what comes up, and don't stop writing, even if you are writing *I don't know* over and over on the page, because after you have done that long enough, a new stream of consciousness will come through. And when it does, write that down too. Don't worry about spelling or punctuation; just write.

After a time of feeling like you're just making it all up as you write, you will feel information start to come through, information that you can tell does not come from your human personality.

I teach every client I meet to do this. And I have been teaching this practice long enough to know that when you look back on this writing, you will be shocked at the fact that you hardly remember writing it and that some of the answers to the questions are nothing short of genius.

Anatomy

As we prepare to enter the Soul House, I want to teach you what the guides have explained about our anatomy. The guides tell me that we, like God, are three-part beings: we are made up of electricity, awareness, and mind.

Electricity. The zero light line is a line I refer to that runs down the center of the body, basically through the spine, like your spinal cord. It connects with the electricity of Source, flows through the body and down into the earth, and then loops back up around and reconnects with Source.

Awareness. I see awareness as a bubble, and in the center of the bubble is a fleck of light—that is the electricity. Awareness goes wherever the mind directs it to; it just witnesses, and I suppose the fleck of light powers it in some way.

Mind. The mind is somewhat more complicated, because within each room of our Soul House, we have so many selves along so many frequencies. This is why it is important to make sure that you are aligned with the zero light line, that your awareness is not in someone else's field but is tucked securely into your own body, and that you have your awareness plugged into the most relevant self, so that the creation process is successful and for your highest and best good.

Assessing Your Spiritual Development

We'll start by figuring out where you stand in your spiritual development.

There are four main phases of spiritual development through which we all cycle as we continue to seek new information. If you're reading this book, you are most likely already in one of them. In fact, I am positive that you are. I just wonder how many times you've cycled through them.

Read through the following four phases to determine where you fall right now, at this moment. Our spiritual journey is never-ending. At any given time, I find myself in one phase or another . . . or even starting right back at the beginning.

Stage One: The Somewhat-Closed Skeptic. You are investigating and searching for truth outside the confines of your reality and beliefs. This stage can take a lifetime, and it is almost always something the soul plans prior to incarnation.

The soul plans the time when stage one begins, and if by free will the human does not begin the spiritual search (whether through religion, science, metaphysics, or other spiritual endeavors), the higher self can invoke an experience where the consciousness is forced to look for answers. This is usually some form of out-of-body experience that the seeker remembers.

We go out of body all the time. We leave daily and we travel nightly to other realms. We just do not remember. But when a soul needs its consciousness to open up and begin searching, it will cause the mind to remember this activity. This, in turn, will lead the human to start asking questions they never would have before. The higher self will also open up the consciousness to ask questions through dreams. Unfortunately some of us must have near-death experiences in order to scare us into stage one. Losing a loved one is the most common reason a human starts on the spiritual-seeking path that leads to this early stage. But if the seeker does not find the answers for which they search, they will lose interest and quit.

If the seeker can be convinced and come to believe that Spirit is real, then they move on to stage two of their development.

Stage Two: The Spiritual Enthusiast. The spiritual enthusiast is very similar to your happy-go-lucky born-again Christian. They want to convert everyone and cannot be convinced of anything other than what they believe in now. Even though it might not be fueled by much common sense, they are enthused. Everything is Spirit! Life is amazing!

The enthusiast thinks that if the wind blows, a spirit is sending a message. If a leaf falls on the ground in front of them, a spirit must be telling them something. These are seekers who see meaningful words and numbers everywhere. They're always looking for the synchronicities in life, so they actually experience them. Intellectually there is not much happening behind stage two. These enthusiasts just feel bliss and joy, and the feeling of believing is so amazing it trumps all else. Unfortunately the bliss eventually fades, and the seeker is left with a feeling of emptiness. So if this happens, the enthusiast either goes back to stage one and becomes a skeptic in search of hard evidence they can believe in, or they maintain their new-found beliefs without the blissful feeling and they go in search of more information to strengthen this belief. This is when they move into stage three. But if the necessary resources, information, and support don't present themselves, these seekers who so strongly believed in God and Spirit will claim temporary insanity and fall back into the way life was before their enlightenment.

Stage Three: The Student. When the spiritual enthusiast becomes the student, real learning begins. The student seeks out information on meditation, energy healing, Reiki, or other healing modalities. They go to classes on intuition or mediumship or that otherwise teach about the nature of humans. They take subconscious reprogramming courses or learn about energy medicine.

These individuals are highly prone to adopting a religion of thought by joining a group of like-minded people to reinforce their beliefs. Without the resources to continue learning in an open, nondogmatic, and unregimented way, many will find themselves joining strict modalities. Most likely the student will find that these stricter groups offer explanations for 3 out of the 10 beliefs that gave them such bliss in stage two, so they will latch on and frame all their spiritual beliefs around this adopted thought matrix, regardless of whether they disagree with the other 7 primary beliefs of the group. To protect these beliefs that are built on the shakiest of grounds, they'll then refuse to look at anything outside them for fear of losing the small amount of belief that is being fostered by this new group or philosophy they've adopted.

Be wary of the third stage. It happens to be the only stage I see myself, my students, and my friends get stuck in. When that happens, the pursuit ends.

But if the student can hold strong to their own beliefs and continue to learn and educate themselves, not only will they likely become a teacher, even if it's just for those closest to them, but they will also move on to stage four.

Ninety-nine percent of spiritual seekers today do not go past stage three. Will you be a part of the one percent who do?

Stage Four: The Spiritualist in Search. Stage four in the spiritual journey is stage one all over again. The only difference is that in stage four the spiritual seeker has a belief in Spirit already instilled in them. Now this seeker is looking for new breakthroughs, new information, and new studies to prove their current beliefs wrong. They hope to find new, more advanced truths.

In this stage the seeker has the experience of knowing their spirits and they likely trust their intuition. So now they begin to ask the tough questions that no one they know has answers for, and the answers begin to come from within or from new combined outside sources as if by magic. In this excitement, stage two kicks back in and the bliss reappears. And this is where the genius inside you, your higher self-knowledge, is truly activated, because now there is no fear of being wrong. There is no fear that you will lose your faith due to contradictory thoughts from your original belief system. This is the endless and glorious search for truth coupled with humility, excitement, and the curiosity of a child.

From here the seeker teaches, but not just as a teacher; they teach as a fellow student. They cannot wait to share with others what they have learned so as to combine what each person has and possibly find more truths. This is a fun stage, but just like anything, it ends—and you loop right back around to stage one.

In this endless soul journey that we are on, we just continue to loop through these four stages over and over. Each time we go through a stage, it looks different and may be about a completely different passion or desire. I personally have gone through these stages with meditation, then with healing, channeling, and healing again, followed by channeling again. I've wanted to know more about the universe, the higher self, and divinity. I love that the journey never stops!

Becoming Aware of Our Awareness

I am sure if you are reading this book, at some point you have heard something like, "We are all just spirits having a human experience, not the other way around." This is true—but our spirit is only one layer of our multidimensional self. The Spirit is the ball of light that connects with Source as previously explained. The same way we have a right brain and left brain, or a liver, or a hand, the spirit is part of our body as a whole, and it is having an experience through the human layer of us. But there is also a layer of self that created that spirit and is experiencing life through *it*, and that is the soul. The soul likewise was created by another layer and is experiencing life through it. This layer beyond soul is what I call the Creator Self.

All those layers make up your *body*; *you* are the awareness that moves around from layer to layer—or room to room in your Soul House. The way you do this is by focusing your attention on where you want to be. It really is that easy!

Discernment

Without a good sense of discernment—that is, a pretty bulletproof technique to determine fact from fiction—you could be fairly lost in this crazy world—no matter which dimension you're inhabiting.

So many authors and teachers say everything on the "other side" is wonderful and beautiful, but I am here to tell you that is not necessarily the case. I am going to educate you about the realms that you cannot see or sense physically but that still affect you just as much as what you experience in the physical realm. I am very protective of my students, and since you are reading this, you are one of my students now.

My plan is to bring you all the things I desperately needed in the beginning, middle, and even end of my spiritual awakening, and all the tools I wish I'd had. I could have avoided a lot of heartache, physical issues, and straight-up frustration at having no clue what I was doing and no one to trust.

In the following exercise, I am going to teach you to discern your truth, not only about books but also about spiritual teachers, gurus, mediums, and other people who seem to know more than you but probably don't. Then, following this easy exercise, if you deem the attunement process to be for your highest and best good, I am also going to start the process that will bring you into contact with your Creator Self. How exciting is that?!

Exercise: Determining Truth

Sit with a straight spine, placing your feet on the ground.

Breathe in light and breathe out any darkness inside in the form of things like stress.

Say, "I am now my awareness."

Imagine you are in a bubble in the center of your brain.

Continue to breathe, pulling all your thoughts, feelings, and energy into the center of your brain. As you do this, the bubble will grow bigger and bigger.

From above you a huge white bubble of light begins to drop down through your head, and as it passes through your head, your bubble merges with it. You are now moving down with it, like being on an elevator into the center of the earth, where the bubble will fill up with earth energy.

When it is full, it will shoot back up to your heart and park itself there.

Now take a book or an item or an idea written on a piece of paper and place it over your heart.

Do you feel expanded or retracted?

Based on how you feel, you will have your answer to whether something resonates with you.

Exercise: Awareness

You must have trust and faith. Be willing to surrender to the benevolence of Source and the process of releasing yourself from negative thoughts and energies that do not serve you. Your commitment is important, since it was by your own choice that you originally came to believe those negative thoughts. But this commitment can only be made if you are *aware* of it, really giving consideration to all that you are doing.

The following exercise is designed to help you find your awareness—something you will need as we journey into Room One and beyond. It works best when done every day for seven to eight days in order to fully connect with and know that you are your awareness.

Sit with a straight spine, placing your feet on the ground.

Ask that your awareness be pulled into a ball of light two feet above your head. Once your awareness is in this ball, draw it into your solar plexus, just above the belly button, below the ribs.

Breathe in and out for a few minutes. Sit and feel this breath and ball fill you.

And now know that you have fully taken ownership of your awareness.

It's that easy.

As easy as the awareness exercise sounds, it is an important one. You need to become aware of that which is you. You are not calling on God in this exercise. You are not calling on angels or guides. You are calling on *your own* wisdom and knowledge. You're asking it to step into your field and into your physical body. You are calling on the part of you that knows why you are here.

As suggested above, if you do this for seven or eight days in a row, you will see a drastic shift in your life. Every day you do this exercise, your awareness aligns you more fully with your life's purpose, whether you are conscious of it or not. This is such an important part of the foundation we are building for our spiritual journey together. Don't forget to write, dictate, journal, or record anything you felt or experienced during this exercise.

Attunement: I Am My I Am

I want you to feel the connection this attunement will create between the real you—that is, your soul's awareness—and Source. I want you to be able to become your soul. Your soul is the one who created the spirit that you are and the one who remembers all your lives and, better yet, knows what will happen in this one. This attunement will bring your awareness into your body and field of consciousness.

At the level of our very core, we are what we think, and our awareness is where our attention is, so before meditation—before any sort of spiritual exercise—it's always good to make sure that you are only you.

What I mean by this is if you have been thinking of your ex-boyfriend constantly for the last day or so, then on a cellular level and within your mind, your body is beginning to react as if it *is* him, in addition to you. It sounds crazy, but remember, we *are* our thoughts! Your energy, thoughts, and emotions go to where your attention is. Awareness is in essence Source experiencing all its creations, so we are all the same awareness. What differentiates our awareness from each other is the consciousness it is attached to—our soul.

In the following exercise, you are not only attuning yourself forever to *you*, but you are also calling back all the little pieces of your awareness that may be causing issues in your life right now. Imagine the difficulty of trying to focus on five video game characters and make sure they all stay alive and function correctly. That is what your brain and soul are having to do if you don't regularly call your awareness back within yourself.

Fill out the following page, and as you do so, the zero point energies programmed into this attunement will begin to connect you with all the layers of yourself and also begin to align you with the zero light line we've been talking about.

You can use this attunement to bring yourself back into alignment at any time.

Day 1: Write your name in each blank below. After filling this out, don't forget to journal! Write out all the things you are expecting to get out of this journey. If you have no expectations, write about what you hope to accomplish in life.

I am _____'s awareness now.

I am _____'s body.

I am _____.

I am _____.

I am _____.

I am _____'s higher self.

I am _____'s spirit.

I am _____'s soul.

I am _____'s I Am now.

I am all that I am *now*!
Thank you! Thank you! Thank you!
It is done.

_____

(Signature)   (Date)

Day 2: Journal about what you are hoping will be released from your life. Then fill in the blanks below.

I am _____'s awareness now.

I am _____'s body.

I am _____.

I am _____.

I am _____.

I am _____'s higher self.

I am _____'s spirit.

I am _____'s soul.

I am _____'s I Am now.

I am MY I am now!

I am all that I am *now*!
Thank you! Thank you! Thank you!
It is done.

_____

(Signature)   (Date)

Day 3: Start with filling out the form below, then sit for about a minute and breathe in through your nose and out through your mouth. When you are feeling relaxed, read all the statements out loud, with your name in each.

Between each statement allow yourself to notice how you feel, and jot that down in your journal. Be aware of any shifts, and write down if you feel anything—or, if you feel nothing, write that down. Continue this practice through the whole attunement list. When you are done, write about how you feel about what you've just experienced, even if it's to complain that you felt nothing.

I am _____'s awareness now.

I am _____'s body.

I am _____.

I am _____.

I am _____.

I am _____'s higher self.

I am _____'s spirit.

I am _____'s soul.

I am _____'s I Am now.

I am all that I am *now*!
Thank you! Thank you! Thank you!
It is done.

_____

(Signature)   (Date)

Attunement: Sink into the Heart Space

Before you can enter your Soul House, you need to be able to access it, and the way to do that is by connecting with, and dropping into the heart space.

The heart in this case is not the physical heart; it is the center of your chest, in the middle of the zero point energy running through you. From there you can access any layer of consciousness you desire—and you can get to that heart space from anywhere, even if you feel stuck.

Close your eyes. Say, "I am my I Am."

Place your hand on your heart and imagine that your awareness is between your hand and the skin of your chest.

Keep your attention there while you relax with a few deep breaths.

Now breathe in through your nose and out through your mouth, making a sighing noise sounding like *haaaa*.

Imagine a bubble just behind you.

Sink back into that bubble, and when you feel it around you, you have made it into your heart space!

I am so happy for you! Congratulations!

Attunement: Align and Center
Your Zero Light Line

Remember that glass elevator we ride up to the Soul House? And remember the cable it is on, the zero light line? We need to make sure your cable is on the right track.

Begin by saying, "I am my I Am."

Close your eyes and imagine a tube of light coming from straight above into your head. This light will shine through the center of your body and down into the earth.

Sit with this light shining through you. Breathe, relax, and imagine pulling all your energy into this tube of light.

Now, once all your energy is contained in this tube of light, sink into your heart space bubble as you did in the previous attunement.

Say, "Zero," and imagine that you are being pulled into the center of your heart space, where you'll find the spark of electricity that represents the zero point energy we all have inside. Let this energy fill your heart space bubble.

Once you feel like you have merged with your bubble, say, "Zero, Source," and imagine a bright light shooting up the tube of light into the zero point of Source (which is shining down on you from above).

Then say, "Zero, ground." Imagine the light now shooting down into the center, or the zero point, of the earth.

Upon doing this you have grounded your awareness into your body and aligned it with all the different layers of mind, body, and soul. You are connected to Source.

Grounding

Before we move forward, we need to make sure you are fully and completely grounded. *Grounding* is a spiritual term, referring to centering your soul in your body, and in turn, connecting your body with the earth. When the connection between your soul, your physical body, and the earth is strong, you are safer and more in touch with your body, your mind, and nature. Your mind remains less distorted by free-floating emotions around you when you're securely grounded, because the neutrality of the unconditionally loving earth can instantly cleanse your energy and keeps your consciousness in your body.

This is something I was told I needed to do when I first started taking Reiki classes. I was told that the deeper our roots are, the taller we can grow without "tipping over" or going crazy. I was told that if I was not grounded, I would not be able to live a balanced life and also do healing and readings. I know I heard what my Reiki master said, but I do not think I actually listened.

I thought if I were grounded, that would mean I wouldn't be able to soar as high as I wanted to! I *liked* being able to see spirits everywhere (for the first year, at least, until it got annoying), and I loved being able to hear and talk to my guides all day every day. But what I have since learned is that, instead, the deeper our energetic roots are, the higher our awareness can travel. If our awareness is not grounded in our own body and we do not use the energy of Source and Mother Earth to staple our awareness to our consciousness, then it is likely our awareness will be *everywhere*! I know so many scattered healers who begin a simple grounding practice and turn into different people almost overnight. This technique took me eight years to try myself, even though the guides asked me to do it for years, every single day. Now, when I teach this technique, I have seen people quit smoking overnight or lose amazing amounts of weight in no time at all. I have seen people quit drinking wine at night or quit sugar altogether. I personally stopped eating candy like it was going out of style, the way I used to. I still sometimes wake in the middle of the night craving sugar, but now I know it is because I need grounding.

Exercise: Grounding

Begin by taking a few relaxing breaths in through your nose and out through your mouth. Let out a sigh to release that extra, pent-up energy that does not belong to you.

Close your eyes and ask yourself where you are. Allow your mind to take you to wherever your awareness is and merge with it.

Say, "I am my I Am." Imagine pulling that ball of light that is you, your I Am, into the center of your brain. Sit and breathe a few more times, relaxing even more.

Imagine a bubble of energy around you, with little tendrils of light shooting out. The tendrils represent every thought you have thought about another person, place, or thing.

When you think about someone or something, a piece of you reaches out and touches the bubble of that some-one or something and exchanges energy; then the next thought ventures out, and so on. After days, months, and years of not clearing these tendrils, the brain becomes a very busy place because it continues to process every single tendril as long as it exists. It's like leaving too many apps open on your iPhone.

Now say, "Come back." Imagine or sense these little tendrils of light being pulled back into your brain, where your consciousness now sits, lined up with your pineal gland, which is the seat of your soul.

Once all the tendrils have been pulled back into your bubble, bring your awareness into your brain. Imagine your awareness dropping down out of your head, through your neck, and into a new bright white bubble of energy that is in the center of your heart space.

Sit with your awareness in the heart for a moment. As you breathe allow the heart space bubble to expand until it floods your entire physical body with its bright white light.

Once your body is full of light, in your mind say, "I am my I Am, and I am now grounded."

Feel your feet rooting into the earth, sinking into the ground, going down through the earth's layers. When your feet are securely grounded in the center of the earth, allow the earth's energy to fill not only your physical body but also a bubble of energy that surrounds you, extending 50 feet up, 50 feet down, and 50 feet to each side, giving you a bubble that is 100 feet across in all directions.

This space that you are creating for yourself will allow you to be in control of your own energy. You will feel a difference immediately. To end this meditation, I bring my awareness to my physical body, wiggle my fingers and toes, and stretch; and then I open my eyes and go about my day.

Exercise: Entering the Soul House

Okay, here we go! You'll recognize the first part of this meditation from earlier in the book.

Close your eyes and breathe in through your nose and out through your mouth to relax.

Say, "Where am I?" Allow your attention to go wherever it is drawn, and then pull your awareness into the center of your chest.

Once your awareness is in the center of your chest, say, "Zero." Imagine there is a platinum or silver-colored ball of light in the center of your chest. Merge your awareness with this.

Say, "Zero, ground," and imagine that light shoots out from this ball, like lightning, down through the center of Mother Earth.

Say, "Zero, Source," and imagine that light shoots out from this ball, like lightning, up to the Source of all creation.

From above, a tube of light emerges, entering the crown of your head and going out through your root, by your tailbone. This tube of light is usually the size of the spine or bigger, and as you work with the aspect of self that is your Creator Self throughout this book, the tube will expand, becoming a stronger channel for your soul's light here on earth.

Sit for a moment and pull all your energy into the center of the tube of light. When this is done, imagine a glass elevator is moving up your zero light line, through your tube of light, toward you, the silver ball of light.

Enter the elevator and sit for a moment imagining what this elevator looks like. Inside the elevator, the doors have mirrors on them, so you can see yourself. There are buttons, but they do not have numbers. There are UP and DOWN buttons, an I AM button, a CREATION ROOM button, a SOUL HOUSE button, and finally a button with your name on it.

From here, press the SOUL HOUSE button, and your elevator will move up into the center of your brain. When the door opens, you will see a hallway with doors down each side. At the end of the hallway, there is a door that represents Room Seven, inside of which are 12 stairs leading up to the Creation Room.

Welcome to your Soul House. The journey we are about to go on will be so much fun!

1

THE PHYSICAL ROOM

The first door in the bright hallway opens onto the Physical Room. Here we are at our most basic and most primal (imagine yourself as a baby, and during your first years of life). In this room you are programmed only to seek out the basics—food, shelter, protection. This is survival of the fittest. Those who live the majority of their lives keeping their awareness in this first room of the Soul House are really into the sensations of the body. Their primary focus is feeling good.

The physical body is the vehicle we experience life through. It is our five senses, the filter through which we experience the natural world. The Physical Room is incredibly important, as it is the only way we can truly remain grounded and therefore able to journey forward. Maintaining this grounding requires eating high-vibration foods and taking advantage of all available help, through both holistic and conventional medicine—even medications for mental health, as necessary. I strongly advocate taking advantage of all that is needed to maintain our physical health.

But of course the physical body is just one layer of our soul, and it is deeply affected by all the other layers. This is why we get sick when we are out of alignment—why we can even die of heartbreak.

This human body, or vehicle, comes equipped with a conscious mind, a subconscious mind, and an ego. All of these are informed by things like our astrological signs, our DNA and ancestry, and so forth. We come preprogrammed, like a computer that already has an operating system in place.

And we continue to be programmed as we move through life, storing beliefs and ideas we pick up, particularly during the first seven years of life when our brain is literally recording everything around it with no filter. Think about it: with no filter at that time, and we trust whatever is given to us—we can't help it! So if, for instance, Mom or Dad hated a certain religion or a certain type of person, we will too, because when we formed that belief, we were too young to dispute it. As we get older, our conscious minds can argue the point, so beliefs like "Intuition and psychic work is evil" or "Money is the root of all evil" are no longer *consciously* accepted—but the *subconscious* has a much harder time breaking through.

These unfortunate programmed beliefs, about things like our relationship to food, our body image, or any traumas stored in our bodies that may cause pain and physical impairments, come with your human vehicle. These can keep you stuck in ways you don't want and don't even understand. So the very first thing we're going to do is begin to dissolve those beliefs that are programmed into your human vehicle that will keep you from moving forward in your spiritual development.

Muscle Testing (Kinesiology)

How will you know what beliefs you have stored in your Physical Room? We are going to use something called kinesiology to test your subconscious mind. This process is honestly so much fun—and it's incredibly useful.

Here's a quick example of the root beliefs I had stored in my subconscious mind:

Root Beliefs	How I Tested
I love myself	Yes
I hate myself	Yes
I love Christians	Yes
I hate Christians	No
I love God	No
I hate God	Yes

Let me tell you, I freaked out when I got that last result! How could I *hate* God? I teach people to connect with God all day, every day!

I asked my guides for answers, and they told me this belief came from my mom. First off, my mom does not hate God either. But she did come from a very strict Baptist family where she couldn't even listen to music other than church music. At some point she equated God with the church. And since the church affected her and her family so deeply, and she has such fear associations with the church, it makes sense that those beliefs would bleed over—and that I would inherit them from her without even realizing it.

When I first started meditating and exploring the other side, I had a very hard time connecting with God. But I didn't understand why until I understood how my subconscious beliefs—some of which weren't even mine to begin with—were getting in the way. After I removed my "I hate God" belief, I finally started to see—to really *see* Spirit and energy. I went from being a good psychic, feeling and sensing things around me, to being a *full-blown clairvoyant*. Who would have thought it would be hate for God that was blocking me?

Mind you, this beliefs test is not foolproof. Before beginning, you need to make sure your awareness is grounded in your I Am and in your heart space and that you are aligned with the zero light line. Otherwise your subconscious (or even some mischievous spirits) could come in and mess with your answers, just for fun.

And you need to use some discernment when choosing which statements to test, particularly with things that might be carrying some emotional weight. If you feel even a tinge of "Oh, I hope the answer is *this*," then your very powerful emotional body will answer the question, overriding your subconscious. One of my friends broke up with her fiancé because her subconscious told her he was cheating on her with *16 women*. Now, this wasn't at all true. The belief was in fact her emotional body remembering an ex-boyfriend, who *had* cheated on her 16 times. Her emotional body showed up, and her subconscious—which knew how much her fiancé loved her—was silenced. This stuff can get tricky, and you really have to pay attention to the statements you test and how you phrase them, and make sure you are allowing your subconscious, and nothing else, to answer. (They ended up getting back together, thank God.)

Exercise: Muscle Testing

This exercise allows you to tap into your subconscious and see what information it has for you that you might not be aware of. Before moving forward with it, make sure you are in your heart space (you may want to use the attunement practice "Sink into the Heart Space" in the previous section of this book), and centered on the zero light line—otherwise the answers you receive from your body may not be accurate.

To begin, stand with your arms by your side and your feet shoulder width apart.

Bring your attention into your body. Imagine filling your entire body with earth energy, drawing it up through your feet.

Say, "My name is (your name)." Allow yourself to sway forward or backward, whichever direction your body goes naturally.

Say, "My name is (someone else's name)." Allow yourself to sway forward or backward, whichever direction your body goes naturally.

Say, "yes, yes, yes," and note which way you sway—to the front or to the back?

Say, "no, no, no," and note which way you sway—to the front or to the back?

Which direction is yes for you? Which direction is no?

Ask a yes-or-no question, one that you know the answer to, like whether you are from a particular town, or whether your car is a certain color, and check to make sure the way you sway matches the true answer to the question.

Exercise: Using the Pendulum

This exercise serves a similar function to the muscle-testing exercise above, and it may serve you better—it depends on how you connect with your subconscious.

Many see the pendulum as very mystical, but it is not. It is simply an item that responds to your energy. You can use a necklace or any other weighted object, though the consensus within the healing community is that wooden pendulums on threads are the most reliable, as they absorb energy from our surroundings less than metals or crystals do.

One note: I have seen people do the craziest things because of a pendulum. This technique can be thwarted if you are not careful to make sure you are centered in your heart space and grounded through your personal zero light line. If your awareness is in someone else's body, you will be getting answers from their energy, not your own.

Say, "I am my I Am." Pull all of your attention and awareness into the center of your chest.

Say, "I am in my heart space."

Say, "Zero."

Say, "Zero, ground."

Say, "Zero source."

Visualize an orb of energy six feet above your head, and allow it to drop down into your space, down into the solar plexus.

Breathe in and out a few times, allowing that energy to expand out from within your body.

Hold your pendulum in your right hand, letting it dangle over your left hand, palm open. Your left hand is the receiving hand. Your energy will respond to your statements, either amplifying or retracting, and this shift will cause the pendulum to move.

Say, "My name is (your name)." Allow the pendulum to sway whichever way it does naturally.

Say, "My name is (someone else's name)." Allow the pendulum to sway whichever way it does naturally.

Say, "show me yes," and note which way the pendulum sways—to the front or to the back? Side to side? Does it swirl around in a circle? Or is it still?

Say, "show me no," and note which way the pendulum sways—to the front or to the back? Side to side? Does it swirl around in a circle? Or is it still?

Which direction is yes for you? Which direction is no?

Knowing which way is yes and which way is no is called coming up with your binary. Different guides will answer in different ways, so you have to set your intention on who you want to communicate with. I always say Higher Self no matter who I want to be communicating with—whether it be my souls, Creator Self, or my I Am.

Now you have discovered which way your body leans when a statement is true and which way it leans when a statement is untrue and/or you have determined the behavior of the pendulum based on the same things.

Imagine the applications of this! There are so many times when we don't know our own truths—but our bodies do. For me, when a client wants me to do a reading but I want to have quality time with my husband and children—in my head I want to do both! I *love* giving readings, and I also love being with my family. So before giving my answer to the client, I give it to an empty room. "Yes," I say. "I would love to do the reading at that time." But if I sway in my *no* direction, I know my body is telling me my statement isn't true.

If I do the reading even though my body said no, then I will run into what we usually call bad luck or the Universe trying to block me from working, in the form of losing my keys, hitting every red light, running out of gas, and so forth. But it is really my own electromagnetic field fighting back because I am going against the flow of what it wanted. Our body really does have its own consciousness, and once we can communicate with our body and know what it wants, we can begin to shift it to wanting what we want, or we can begin to follow what it wants, and live a more harmonious life mentally, emotionally, and spiritually.

Keep the Water Flowing

In Room One, it is important to note that as physical beings, we are energy in its densest form. And like all energy, we need a conductor to be able to get anywhere. What is the best conductor of energy? Water. What is the human form made up of? Water. It is said that an adult body is 50 to 65 percent water. Infants and children are made up of a whole lot more, but they're a lot purer than us adults, right?

So the first thing I want you to do is pour yourself a glass of water. Actually, don't stop at one. Keep going. Drink water. Lots of water. The more water you drink, the better your energy will be, the higher your vibration, and the more intuitive you'll become. Water is a huge part of what we are, and we need to stay hydrated.

I recommend, as do most nutritionists, dieticians, and health-care professionals, that you drink at least half your body weight in ounces of water every day. So let's start now. Go get some water, take a break, take a sip. When you come back, we'll start conducting energy!

Oh, and don't forget to journal. Even drinking water can be part of your record keeping. Mark down how many ounces of water you are drinking daily. Just bringing awareness to your water consumption will likely increase it.

The Taming of the Ego

Our subconscious, unaware behavior is frequently tied up with the ego, that other part of us that came preprogrammed in our physical vehicles. It is a very strong—and loud—human attribute. It's certainly something I struggle with—my ego was completely in charge for years. It still takes over sometimes. In fact, it's a daily challenge to maintain the working relationship between my ego, my Creator Self, and my soul, all sharing this body that is Marisa. Let me tell you a story—it's one I find fairly embarrassing now, but it certainly illustrates the power ego has over us.

I had spent a lovely day lying on the couch, reading and watching television, just relaxing in comfy clothes. When it was time to leave to go to a class in San Diego, I started driving, easy and calm as could be. But then, halfway there, I started panicking. I remembered that at the previous class, I had experienced a huge epiphany, meeting my higher self for the first time, breaking down crying, telling stories of my addiction, and so on. Everyone had been so supportive, but now I was embarrassed. I pulled off the highway, stopped in at Nordstrom, and bought a suit. I put it on in the car and walked into class 15 minutes late, just so everyone could see how fancy I was, how important I was, wearing my suit and doing important things with my day (certainly not some former addict who had been so vulnerable in front of them). Then I excused myself to the bathroom to change into "comfy clothes"—the very same clothes I had been wearing when I left my house only two hours before.

I have to laugh at myself now, but I am sharing this moment because I have so much compassion for the Marisa who thought she needed to impress people, people who clearly accepted her for who she was already. In fact, they probably liked the comfy Marisa more. But my ego was in charge nearly 24/7 back then, and it was constantly announcing, "I am better than all of you, and I work so much harder."

Once we know what our ego's voice sounds like, we can ignore it and eventually learn to tune it out.

So promise me this: As you move through this book, make sure you check your ego at the door. Notice when it speaks and make note of it in your journal. The more you do this, the more acquainted you will become with this little three-lettered pest, and the more you will learn to keep it under control.

Projections

Once we become more aware of our ego, we can recognize that those around us act as our mirrors—what we notice most in others is often merely a reflection of ourselves. We feel these reflections strongly in our bodies; they echo through our physical selves in Room One. And when we feel angry at others, that is often just a projection of our anger at ourselves.

The best way to understand your mood each day is to actually slow down for a moment within your mind and listen to the things you are accusing everyone else of doing. More often than not, it's something you know *you* would do.

I used to have *ridiculous* road rage. I would shake with it. I literally drove around with the attitude that *Everyone is out to get me, so I must cut them off and slam on my brakes to get back at them for not respecting me.* I was convinced that people were cutting in line to get in front of me; they were speeding past me and riding my tail simply to bug me. I felt like every time someone passed me on the freeway, they were challenging me.

Of course, when you say it out loud like that, it sounds silly. And one day after learning about projection, I finally asked myself: *Who is it that I am wanting to challenge? What in me is making me so angry?* That is when I realized that I was playing out all of my issues in life with people I did not know on the freeway, because I would never have to see them again and I would never have to actually get to the bottom of why I felt the way I did. I realized I was reacting to a murmuring loop of criticism in my mind, full of things my father used to nitpick at when he taught me to drive. I was deflecting that criticism onto other drivers. After this revelation, I was able to address the root cause of my anger.

When I learned about projection and I started being more aware, I was able to turn off my road rage. If someone cut me off, instead of assuming they were doing it just because they could, I decided to say, "Oh wow, I should let them pass me. What if their wife is in labor?!" It made such a difference. It had been exhausting being such a defensive person—my shoulders and back and neck ached, and I was just a tense ball of muscle by the time I got where

I was going. I am so grateful that Source drives with me to work now.

The mirror of the human race shows the positive as well as the negative, so this reflection and projection also goes for the things you admire in others. Those things often turn out to be qualities you have in abundance—you just might not be aware of it or willing to see those things in yourself.

Taking this a step further, the people you admire can give you an idea of what your soul's path is. Bringing my awareness to the people I admire has actually changed my course a few times—whether they were authors, spiritual teachers, healers, or even stay-at-home soccer moms who handled their own messy lives in a way I wanted to emulate.

Exercise: What Am I Projecting?

Let's bring your awareness to your projections—both negative and positive. The following lists will give you an idea of things you may be projecting. This will help you know how to move forward.

Either here or in your journal, jot down five things you cannot stand about others:

1. _____

2. _____

3. _____

4. _____

5. _____

Now write five things you really love or admire in others:

1. _____

2. _____

3. _____

4. _____

5. _____

And now ask yourself, "When was the last time you exhibited any of the above behaviors—positive and negative?" List a memory for as many of these qualities as you can.

_____

_____

_____

_____

_____

_____

When you become more aware of your projections, you can change so much. You can change your own behaviors—which will serve as positive actions for others to reflect back to you—and you can change your own perceptions, choosing to see positive intentions instead of the negative ones you yourself were bringing.

How Your Gripes Can Change Your Life

I want to ask you to keep a "gripe list." It's based on the same concept as the projection exercise, but it takes you a little deeper. The gripe list is a list of things that bother you about me, you, other people, even the teachings in this book.

These lists are for you and you only. No one else needs to see them at all. They will help you figure out how you are triggered each and every day by your own projections. They will help you see that a lot of what you think of as drama thrown at you by other people happens only to be a piece of you that is still young and learning, a piece that is frequently stuck here in Room One.

Here's an example of my own: Last week I was listening to an audiobook recommended by a really good friend of mine. She said the subject matter was *amazing* and the author's teachings *totally* reminded her of me. So of course I downloaded the book—but I couldn't even make it through the first five minutes. That girl drove me crazy! I had to turn it off.

A couple days later, my guides suggested I go back to that audiobook, to practice what I preach and pay attention to my own gripes. Well, I had a *lot* of gripes on that list. But I'm only going to go over two—otherwise we might be here forever!

Gripe #1: She is *loud, sarcastic,* and *annoying* because she *thinks she's cool.*

Gripe #2: She is *not acting professional.* How dare she do that when she has such a great opportunity to get her message out?

Now, if just writing down what bugs us were it for the gripes exercise, that wouldn't help any of us get very far! At this point, we *could* simply walk away, leaving our negativity and criticism as just that. But what can these gripes teach us? What could my gripes teach *me*?

Exercise: Addressing Your Gripe

Sit in a quiet place.

Say, "I am my I Am."

Visualize a bright bubble of light in the center of your chest. Pull all your attention into that bubble. Sit for a moment while your attention is collected in this heart bubble.

When you feel relaxed and centered, say, "How old is the me that is griping about (your gripe)?"

Whatever comes to your mind first is your answer.

Reflect on this now. Think back to that age. What were you like? What was life like? Journal about it. Think about the reasons your inner child or young adult is griping. Think about the defining circumstances or emotions in your life at that time. What is your perception of the other person or thing that is bothering you?

Imagine each reason and perception written out on a little piece of paper.

Imagine a fishbowl in front of you. Put the pieces of paper inside it.

Now say this affirmation prayer:

I am my I Am and I am free of all reflections, projections, and judgments from my _____ -year-old self. I ask that Source send her/him all energies, frequencies, thoughts, or emotions required to facilitate a complete healing and make her/him whole and complete.

Then imagine the brightest light possible pouring down over you and the fishbowl in front of you. After the light has covered you completely, imagine it dissolving the fishbowl and all the papers in it.

Say, "Thank you."

Repeat this process with any other gripes you may have.

And the Results Are . . .

Here is what it looked like when I performed the gripe exercise on my own:

Gripe #1: She is *loud, sarcastic,* and *annoying* because she *thinks she is cool.*

Who is griping? My 15-year-old inner child.

Why is she griping? Not sure exactly why, but that is when I switched schools and felt like I had no friends.

What is the perception? I think this author is insecure, so she is trying to cover it up by being sarcastic and loud and cool so no one will know she's really afraid.

Gripe #2: She is *not acting professional.* How dare she do that when she has such a great opportunity to get her message out?

Who is griping? My 27-year-old self.

Why is she griping? I don't know why she is griping, but that is when I ended up in court for doing drugs and then was sent off to rehab because I showed up wearing flip-flops, jeans, and a tank top. I did not take anything I was going through seriously.

What is the perception? I perceive that the author doesn't know how to be professional, so she behaves in the exact opposite way, rather than trying and failing miserably—like when you don't want to look like you're trying too hard to look good, so you only put a little makeup on and dress like you don't care, even though you really do. It's better to look like you didn't try than to look as if you had tried and failed.

After doing this exercise, I went back to the audiobook and replayed it. This time I didn't hear the same "nails on chalkboard" voice I heard before. Instead I heard how awesome the content was—I learned so much from her! And to top it off, she didn't sound loud after all. I actually tried to hear her the way I had heard her before I did the exercise, and it was impossible. "She" was different! In fact, I found her to be perfectly professional and that what she was doing was having fun, so in turn, I was having fun listening to her.

Lesson Learned: I was seeing myself in the author, and after healing that piece of me, I no longer perceived her as doing anything wrong. In addition, I no longer have a need to be loud and sarcastic when I feel insecure or feel others may be judging me. I am now confident, strong, and whole. I can remove the sarcasm from my teachings, since that was clearly just an attempt to cover up my insecurities and fear of being judged. Plus, I no longer feel the need to be overly professional in my lessons when unconsciously I wish I were making them more fun.

So if something I write in this book or someone in your daily life really hits hard, good or bad, jot it down. Later, when you have time to reflect on it, or when it's time to journal or meditate, follow the simple exercise above. After you get the hang of this, you will be able to catch yourself griping and heal the inner child who is causing the irritation. Who would've thought that complaining could actually change your life?

Leaving Room One

Our bodies have so much to tell us if we only listen. They tremble, ache, and echo with all the information that drifts around the different rooms. As such, our bodies are hardly ever where the source of the problem is; they just pass the message along. So let's venture back out into that bright hallway and see what's behind door number two.

2

THE EMOTIONAL ROOM

This is a tough room for many of us, as it's full of emotions. It's human nature to slam that door shut, jog on by, and never look back. But not today. Today we are going to walk into that room, get comfy, and really spend some time with our emotions.

Emotion, just like *everything* else, is simply energy.

Take a moment and think back to a time when you were in a great mood, totally loving life, and then you walked into a room, and *wham*, just like that, you felt edgy or angry for no apparent reason. This has happened to me countless times; sometimes so powerfully that I would fall into a depression. In fact, this phenomenon had a lot to do with my 16-year battle with addiction.

Yep, Room Two is scary all right.

But emotions aren't so scary once you begin to understand what they are and what is causing them. Emotions are direct reflections of your or others' energy.

Here's how it works: Let's say it's date night at home. All is great, but you need to run out and buy butter to drizzle on top of your freshly popped popcorn. You cheerfully trot on out to the store while your happy date patiently waits for your return. While at the store, you find yourself in the line of a checkout clerk whose spouse is furious with her. You don't know this—she doesn't share it with you—in fact, you hardly even speak to her. You pay for your butter, smile, and wave good-bye.

Five minutes later, you walk into your house, and all of a sudden you get this nagging feeling that your date is furious with you! "Did I take too long? Did I buy the wrong butter? Does he not want to watch the movie I chose?" And while you're spiraling like this, your emotions start to build. You become defensive, because after all, you know you didn't do anything wrong!

Although you can't seem to think of why he could be mad, your mind will continue to scan for reasons, trying to come up with an explanation for this new negative energy you have—the energy you absorbed from the cashier.

The mind is programmed to process energy; that is, it is up to your mind to find a person, place, or memory that matches any energy it encounters. In the example above, your mind is trying to place the cashier's energy, and now you begin to just *know* without a doubt, that you are in big, big trouble, with a capital *T.* You even have a sick feeling in the pit of your stomach—that's Room One coming in to join the party.

After nine years of working as a spiritual healer, and having gone through this so many times myself (oh, how many fights I have had with my husband that weren't even our fights to begin with!), I have come to believe that this is how most fights begin—not only between lovers and family, but in the workplace and in public as well. These fights tend to revolve around messy energy and assumptions being passed between unsuspecting people. All it takes is one person assuming one thing based on a feeling they get and then the situation spirals out of control. You all know what they say happens when you assume, right?

Let's revisit that date night. If you don't realize quickly that you picked up the cashier's energy when you were checking out, you will most likely start to give your date the silent treatment. He will react to that unfair silence and turn around and assume you *have* done something wrong. He will take it one step further by starting to accuse you (either in his head or out loud) of whatever you have supposedly done wrong.

Do you see where this is going?

This can happen with *anything*, at any time, and in any place—but there are ways to deal with it. Using a tool like the Snow Globe visualization can help you protect yourself.

The Snow Globe

The Snow Globe has become the center of all my spiritual teachings. I have found the Snow Globe to be the single most effective tool I know of to hold and keep our energies pure and connected to our I Am.

The Snow Globe is *you*. It is your energy field, and it allows you to see and feel what is going on in your world—at all levels—at any given moment.

Here's how it came to be: In December of 2011, I was at my weekly mediumship class. Before the lesson each week, the teacher would lead a 15-minute meditation to get everyone in the right frame of mind to learn and be open to the spirit world. He'd lead us into a big ball of light and then into a land where we would meet our guides. Every week most of the students in class would have some amazing experience and report back details of who their guide was and where their adventures had taken them.

Meanwhile, I was struggling to sit still through the 15-minute meditation. I would stare at the black backs of my eyelids and obsess about how much I sucked at meditation. I never met a guide! The whole thing seemed stupid. But I wanted so badly to learn to communicate with the spirits I had been seeing outside of meditation.

Then finally, a week before Christmas, I met my guide. As the teacher led us into the ball of light, I started to make out the silhouette of a man. He was in all white, with fur around his collar and the bottom of his robe. He was holding a staff, and he had a huge white beard and long, wavy white hair. It was Santa! No, not the fat Coca-Cola Santa who wears red, but the one who wears solid white and is trim and wise looking.

I thought, *Really?! My freaking guide is* Santa*?!*

Santa walked up to me and said, "I know you're sad. We hear your cries. Please don't hurt yourself anymore. It hurts us to see how much you think you hate yourself."

Then he reached out his hand, which suddenly grew to the size of the room. In his hand he held a huge Snow Globe, and I was in the center of it.

He said, "You are a Snow Globe, and I have you in the palm of my hand. We love you so much, and we will never let you go."

Then a huge beam of light from straight above the Snow Globe came pouring in through the glass, zapping the me inside with so much light it was blinding. Although I literally felt like I was in the Snow Globe, with all the snowflakes and water swirling around me, the me in "real life" could feel my back pain releasing, my head tingling, and my left eye twitching. I was finally experiencing an adventure like the others in class had experienced in the past. I was so excited! I never wanted to leave my Snow Globe in Santa's hand and return to reality. I left class that night feeling joyous for the first time in years.

About a month later, my dad and I got together so I could give him a healing for the first time. Before beginning, I was filled with fear. I finally felt I had found my calling, but my father was—is—a traditional Christian, and I didn't want him to think I'd gone crazy or to discourage me in any way. I was finally sure about my place in the world and knew with every piece of my being that I wanted to channel and heal people. I didn't want his disapproval to jeopardize that.

I was taught that if I said a prayer of protection, I'd be protected, but this time, unlike all the other times I had said such a prayer, I did not feel protected. I only felt fear. But then I heard, "You are a Snow Globe, dear one; we love you; you are in the palm of my hand, and I will never let you go."

My dad's whole house turned into a Snow Globe in my mind, and a shower of white light came pouring down over us. I felt peace, and once again, so much joy.

The session went amazingly well, and since then my dad has been my biggest fan and supporter.

Attunement: The Snow Globe

Before you can use your Snow Globe, you have to get yourself into it. Let's get you attuned. Please say:

If it is for my highest and best good and in alignment with my real self and true soul's mission to be attuned, I now ask my higher self to allow this attunement to the Snow Globe and the energies used in it. Thank you.

Find a place where you can be alone and can concentrate for at least five minutes. As always, make sure that you are aligned with the zero light line and are firmly in your heart space.

Close your eyes and breathe deeply, in and out.

Say, "I am (your name) now," to bring your awareness into your own space.

Say, "Where am I right now?" Your awareness will most likely shift to somewhere other than in your own head. It could be right outside your head, at the office, or a thousand miles away on vacation somewhere.

Say, "Come back." Imagine a little version of yourself moving toward your mind, toward that bright ball of consciousness behind your third eye. Merge little you into that bright ball. Once you can imagine that *you* are in the middle of your brain, just breathe and feel what it is like in there. Is it calm, busy, noisy, quiet, hot, cold?

Imagine there is another ball of light, this one two feet above your head. What color is it? Make sure it is directly above you, and then will it to drop straight down into your head. When it is surrounding your awareness in the middle of your brain, imagine you are in that ball, inside your brain, protected. What does your brain feel like now? Have things slowed down or sped up? Is the temperature the same? There are no right or wrong answers, and it may be different every time.

Say, "I am now a Snow Globe." Imagine you are a statue in the middle of a Snow Globe. What does that statue feel like? What does it look like from all directions? What is the color, shape, texture?

What is the water around the statue like? Is it goopy or thin? If you were swimming through the water, would it be clear or murky? What are the snowflakes in your Snow Globe like? What color are they? What size? Spend a moment experiencing and imagining what your Snow Globe feels and looks like.

What about the outside of the Snow Globe? Is it small or large? Is the glass thick or thin? Is it cracked or intact, clean or dirty? Let your imagination run wild.

Look up now. Imagine a huge shining Snow Globe above you, hovering six feet above your head. From it there is liquid light dropping down through your Snow Globe, into your head, and pouring down through your heart space to the earth below you. This is the zero light line.

As this energy pours into the bubble that holds your awareness, that bubble begins to expand. It gets bigger and bigger, transmuting all darkness, all attachments, anything that is not you, cleaning and clearing. As the bubble is infused with light and energy, the Snow Globe around you clears along with it—the water becomes crystal clear, the snowflakes turn white, and any cracks or distortions in your glass are instantly repaired.

Say, "I am now protected." A beautiful golden liquid pours down over your Snow Globe like thick paint, coating it entirely. As the golden coat dries, you are cleansed, clear, and safe in your I Am, in your Snow Globe.

Housekeeping with the Snow Globe

Now that you're in your Snow Globe, let's start some housekeeping in this dreaded, emotional Room Two. Let's get rid of any snowflakes that aren't yours and make you pure and clean and bright and shiny and brand-new again.

Imagine that the snowflakes in your Snow Globe are any of the following emotions, or make some up yourself.

Abandoned	Cowardly	Dramatic
Abused	Crazy	Embarrassed
Accused	Critical	Emotional
Addicted	Criticized	Empty
Afraid	Cruel	Entitled
Aggravated	Deceptive	Envy
Aggressive	Defeated	Exhausted
Angry	Defensive	Exploited
Anxious	Depressed	Extravagant
Argumentative	Desperate	Fake
Arrogant	Destructive	Fatigued
Avoidant	Detached	Fearful
Betrayed	Disappointed	Foolish
Bitter	Discontent	Furious
Blamed	Discounted	Gloomy
Bored	Discouraged	Grieving
Bullied	Disgusted	Guilty
Burdened	Dishonest	Heartbroken
Busy	Displeased	Heavy
Cheated	Distrusting	Helpless
Compromised	Disturbed	Hopeless
Conceited	Dominating	Horrible
Conflicted	Doubtful	Hostile
Controlled	Drained	Humiliated

Hurt	Nervous	Shattered
Impatient	Obligated	Shy
Impulsive	Obsessed	Shocked
Inaccurate	Outraged	Struggling
Inadequate	Overlooked	Stupid
Incomplete	Overwhelmed	Suspicious
Indebted	Overworked	Threatened
Indifferent	Pained	Terrified
Indignant	Persecuted	Tired
Insecure	Pessimistic	Tortured
Intimidated	Poor	Trapped
Intense	Prejudiced	Traumatized
Intolerant	Pressured	Ugly
Irrational	Prideful	Unappreciated
Irresponsible	Provoked	Uncomfortable
Irritated	Punished	Unfulfilled
Jealous	Put down	Unhappy
Judged	Rebellious	Unnerved
Lazy	Regretful	Unplugged
Let down	Rejected	Unsupported
Lonely	Repressed	Unwanted
Mad	Resentful	Unworthy
Manipulated	Responsible	Upset
Mean	Ridiculed	Uptight
Mediocre	Rude	Used
Melancholy	Ruthless	Vengeful
Miserable	Sad	Weak
Misunderstood	Sarcastic	Weird
Moody	Scared	Worthless
Mournful	Sensitive	Worried
Needy	Self-centered	
Neglected	Shamed	

You can use your Snow Globe to clear all these and more. All it takes is awareness and intention. Allow any of the emotions above that resonate with you in this moment to color the snowflakes in your Snow Globe. Really see and feel them; feel their texture. And then imagine the white light of Source shining down to extinguish the feelings you want to get rid of, zapping and clearing each and every one of those discolored snowflakes, until your Snow Globe is clean and bright.

Leaving Room Two

Emotions—ours, and those of the people around us— are incredibly powerful. They can teach us so much about our own experience. But when we ignore them, we allow them to control us. If, instead, we use our awareness and our understanding of the energy of emotions, we can completely change our experience in this life.

And now let us step back into the hallway and enter Room Three.

3

THE MENTAL BODY ROOM

As the door of Room Three swings open, you step into the mental realm—but it is not mental in the way you would think. Yes, the intellectual mind feeds this room unconsciously in the sense that it adds to the intellect's store of learned data. But this is not the stuff you learn in school or the stuff you learn consciously. This room stores everything you experience—and everything you do not experience as well. This room is what string theorists speak of, with multiple realities existing at the same time. This room houses the you that exists outside of time. This you experiences and learns things that your conscious mind does not pick up on.

For example, when you were in school, there were times when you would tune your teacher out and day-dream. You would get yanked back into reality by the bell ringing or the boy who had a crush on the girl who sat next to you hitting you with a spitball or a note you needed to pass. The piece of you that was "gone" was your conscious mind, or what I have referred to throughout this book as your I Am awareness. While your I Am is out flying around on unicorns, or doing whatever it is you do when you daydream, your other layers of self are still in your human body and brain.

This is where the mental body becomes very useful. The mental body stays for the lecture and records everything word for word, but it does so without emotion, without a filter of discernment. It is your I Am that discerns.

When your I Am discerns in combination with the second room, fear usually creeps in and makes you irrational. Even when you discern with the high vibration part of your emotions, you may do things that are bad for you because you are happy and think that nothing can bring you down.

But when you are in your Mental Body Room, you are just data. Emotions do not exist. The Mental Body Room acts much like the subconscious mind, but it is the layer of self that the Creator Self programs, the same way a computer would be programmed with both data and software that runs that data.

In this room we have the Divine Mind, which is all the information from all of our lives past that our Creator Self wants us to have stored away. In this room we also have our soul plan, our archetype, our astrology sign, our gender, our nationality . . . it is the *blueprint of us* when we enter this life. It is our identity as a human being in this lifetime. The second we are born, this room begins gathering data and storing it. The amazing thing is that you can place your I Am awareness inside this room, which allows you to pull from it information about lives past, about the future, about your present situation—you can even ask it for advice. The mental body is kind of like Siri! If you do not ask, it will not answer, but if you do ask, you will receive answers with information beyond your wildest dreams.

The other thing I love about this room and the mental body is that it is our intuition in a 3D reality. It has all our psychic or intuitive abilities. Before opening this book, you may have had a strong sense that you could be a medium or that maybe you are an empath who is clairsentient. Or maybe you were like me when I started, and you feel you could never possibly have abilities that are so amazing, but you are going to read and study as much as you can in hopes of someday becoming a channeler. Regardless of who you are and what you have done, where you have been, what your family is like, and how you were raised to look at spiritual gifts, I am excited to tell you that your Divine Mind in your third room has *all* these abilities, so take your pick! Which ones do you want to develop? By merging with and becoming this piece of yourself, the five senses you know as your human senses become able to pick up on subtle energies around us, because the vibration of the mental body is much higher than the physical body. Cool, huh?

I can safely say that when the planet was only able to be aware of the first three rooms, this was the higher self as we understood it. But now we can go beyond. I communicated with my mental body as my higher self for a long time. But I realized I was just looking at one layer of my body, believing it was my higher self, and then my *real* higher self, my Creator Self, stepped forward. I started communicating with the Creator Self instead—and my world has never been the same. That being said, the mental body is a great place to start. By tuning in to this Divine

Mind—this layer of your soul body that has never fallen asleep in class and pays attention to everything your boss says—by beginning to align yourself with this piece of you, your life will change!

This self will appear to the human mind in meditation or during spiritual awakening as Jesus or some other respected teacher. I have actually had at least a hundred people I do not know, but who have heard my radio show, tell me that I appear to them in dreams and help them by taking them on journeys in their meditations. They say my higher self healed them during their sessions. That freaked me out the first time I heard it! I thought, *How could that be happening without my knowledge?* I hoped it was not some spirit posing as me to get into someone's energy. I asked the guides, and they said it was not really me at all—it was that person's own mental body appearing as someone they trust to help them through issues, using data stored in the Divine Mind to heal them and bring them back into alignment with their Divine Blueprint.

The work of our mental body guiding us can appear to be a miracle, because when we realign with our Divine Blueprint, we can heal some illnesses that we walked into blindly but of our own free will. When we are thrown off our path, the Creator Self pulls out all the stops to make sure we get back on track. If having a layer of ourselves appear as someone we will actually listen to aids in our healing or shifting, then why not?

Before we move into this chapter's exercises, I want you to remember that while Room Three is incredibly powerful, it is not perfect. It is a perfect version of yourself *as you are now*, but you can grow beyond even that as you proceed further into this book!

Why do we need to shift this piece of us if it is perfect? Our soul programs lessons that need to be learned into this self, and with the way the planet is shifting, many are blowing through their lessons! Because we have not learned to bring our conscious awareness past this room, the mental body is outdated—it has not caught up to the 4D awakening that the planet has experienced. So while we are in this room, we are going to ask your Creator Self to update your Divine Blueprint, and then we are going to align you with your Divine Mind!

Exercise: Updating the Divine Blueprint

Say, "I am my I Am."

Say, "I am now in my glass elevator."

Say, "Zero," and witness as the zero light line runs through your spine from above and out the bottom of the elevator.

Say, "Tube of light," and witness as the tube of light drops down from above, going through your body and out the bottom of the elevator.

From above, a huge bubble of searing hot, burning white light drops down into the elevator, into your crown, and then into your solar plexus. Breathe in and out a few times with the intention to expand the bubble out as far as it wants to expand.

Now look into the mirrors on the inside of the elevator doors and say, "I am now my Divine Blueprint. Show me what I look like." Then look. What do you see? Let your imagination run wild!

Now say, "I am my I Am, and I command that my Creator Self and Source update my Divine Blueprint now."

From above, a huge ball of energy drops down into your elevator and ignites you with light.

Watch as your image in the mirror changes. It does not matter what you see as long as you see yourself change. (If you don't change, it means you did not need an update to begin with!)

Once you are done updating your Divine Blueprint, say, "Zero," and you will go back to your body, ready to open your eyes and go about your day.

You can update your Divine Blueprint for isolated reasons, such as finances or love. In this case you would say, "I am now my Divine Blueprint for love," and then do the exercise exactly the same way.

Attunement: Activating the Divine Mind and Decalcifying the Pineal Gland

Start this exercise by grounding yourself, alone in your Snow Globe, and as always, align yourself with the zero light line in your heart space.

Say, "I am my I Am."

Bring your awareness into the center of your brain, which is where your pineal gland is located. This is often referred to as the third eye, or the inner seeing. We're going to decalcify and activate this area in the highest and best possible way, so that you may begin to connect with your soul's genius.

Imagine a ball of energy, a ball of light, there in the center of your brain. Say, "Take me into the center of my soul's intelligence in the pineal gland," or just imagine that you're there.

Now allow the ball of light to drop down through your head, down through your throat, down through your chest, along your spine, through your torso, all the way down the bottom of your tailbone, and out your root chakra at the base of the spine. This ball of electricity that is you will continue down into the earth, where earth energy will begin to heal anything in you that needs to be healed, seen or unseen, known or unknown.

At the center of the earth, there are beautiful silver, aquamarine, and golden energies. These are Mother Earth's energies, and this is where your physical body was created. Allow these neutral earth energies to surround your ball of electricity, healing you and creating another bubble of light around you.

When the electricity that is you is completely surrounded with these beautiful earth energies of unconditional love, hope, peace, joy, commitment, and loyalty to yourself and others, you'll automatically begin to rise up.

Let your ball of light rise back to where you came from, going up the same channel through the earth. As you approach your physical body, you return back up through the floor. As you enter your physical body, the beautiful earth energies fill your feet, your legs, your hips. They fill your abdomen, your torso, your chest, going into your arms and fingertips. They fill your shoulders, releasing the weight you carry for yourself and others—releasing it and sending it back to Mother Earth. Then you bring this beautiful energy from the earth up into your head, allowing it to completely fill your brain. This will bring the little ball of electricity that is you back to the center of your brain.

Say, "Yes." Release all fears about activating your intuition, all fears about activating a connection. Release all fears that you may be harmed or hurt if you are intuitive, able to connect with things that other people cannot see or feel or define.

Your relationship to the Divine Mind accompanies you all day, wherever you go. You can block frequencies or you can open yourself to them.

Exercise: Messages from the Divine Mind

Now that you are attuned, imagine that your connection to the Divine Mind is a ball of energy floating five or six feet above you. What color is it? Is it green? Pink? Even if you're not a visual person, you may "hear" or "feel" a color. Just allow yourself to imagine its color and size and then visualize this orb of light dropping down into the top of your head and completely surrounding your head—a big bubble of light.

Just sit for a moment and allow any messages to download. You've plugged in your hard drive; now let's see what's on there. You can ask specific questions, or you can say things like, "Show me an image of something that will represent the answer to my question about whether I should take this job or not, or should stay in this relationship, or should have a child." Without judgment, just watch, feel, and listen to what comes through. If you see nothing or feel nothing, this is okay too. By just sitting, you're allowing the information into your field without disruption.

Now imagine this bubble of light around your head beginning to shrink into the center of your mind, so that it is wrapped perfectly around the ball of electricity that is in the center of your brain. Once it is wrapped around that electricity, this energy shoots directly up out of your head, securing a connection to Source, and directly down through your body, out from your root, securing a connection to earth. Feel what it feels like to be connected to the earth. To Source.

If you have any remaining worries or anxieties, ask that they be released into the earth or into Source. Release yourself from the obligation to know everything, to be right—because this need is what blocks most of us from our intuition. Infuse your being with the ability to just have fun and play like a child, even if you're asking serious questions. Move the ego out of the way. Tell it, "We're just playing games right now; we're just having fun. Go ahead and take a seat."

Bring your awareness back to your physical body, beginning with your hands. If you like, you can visualize that light energy you called into your mind shooting from your mind into your hands.

And now, with that energy and awareness in your hands, sit and write or type—whatever you prefer. Don't bother with punctuation; don't bother with handwriting. Just write what comes to mind and remember that nothing is perfect; nothing is right and nothing is wrong. Just write.

Never take this too seriously or you will surely block the frequencies. The ego just loves to block this kind of fun. If you find yourself wanting to ask questions about investments or serious medical issues for yourself or others, this exercise is not a good one to use. Using something where your brain is not involved at all would be more suitable. Your Divine Mind likes to have a good time!

Exercise: Grounding the Divine Mind into the Body with Neutral Earth Energy

Now that you are attuned to your Divine Mind, you can use this meditation technique to access it at any time, and to clear and cleanse all dimensions of yourself, grounding into the first three rooms in advance of venturing forward, and keeping your upper-dimensional self attached to your physical body. This will be very useful as we journey onward.

Stand, relaxed, with your feet shoulder-width apart and your hands in prayer position. Close your eyes. Say, "I am my I Am."

Bring your awareness to the center of your brain, where there is a shining ball of light.

In your mind say, "Come back," bringing any pieces of your awareness that might be out and about into your pineal gland.

Breathe deeply into this space in your brain for five seconds. This space will expand as all the thoughts you have scattered throughout your reality return to you. On each exhale, release that which is blocking you from collecting yourself and tuning in to this pure awareness within your brain.

When you feel as if the shining ball has expanded and is the size of your brain, take a final deep breath and relax your shoulders, allowing your arms to softly rest at your sides.

Now bring your awareness to a shining ball in the center of your chest. Allow the ball in your brain to drop down and connect with the ball in your heart. When the two merge, allow them to expand out until their light fills your entire body and creates a bubble around you. This is your auric field.

Next, bring your awareness to the soles of your feet, imagining little upside-down tornados emanating from them and pointing into the earth. These twisters pull in the zero point energy that is connected to the earth.

Return to your breath. With each inhale imagine earth's energy flowing up through your body. With each exhale visualize earth's energy swirling into the bubble around you, blending with your energy, clearing and balancing you.

In your mind say, "Zero," to call in the zero light line. From directly above you, a bolt of Source light will shoot down through the top of your head, through your pineal gland, through your heart space, and down through your center to connect with the earth.

Feel how it is to be in complete alignment with your Divine Mind, with the earth, and with Source.

Leaving Room Three

It is very important to do exercises like the above, particularly as you start to develop your spiritual gifts. If you begin to tune in to your higher levels of consciousness without a clear mind, you might mistake your subconscious mind for your Creator Self or another entity, and you may see or feel some very untrue things that you think are coming from beyond the human realm. You may think you had a particular past life, when in reality it was a movie you saw when you were five and stored in your brain. You may think you are reading the future, when it's really just something you worry will happen; but since you thought it, it is now stored within your brain.

The mental body has so much truth and wisdom, but it holds all that information within the confines of our mind's interpretation. It is very important to remember that the mental body does not know all, as it is skewed by interpretation and the subconscious.

We are about to move to a level higher than most people experience in their lifetime. Step back into the hallway, and let's move to the fourth dimension.

4

THE ASTRAL ROOM

When we begin to allow ourselves to move past our subconscious, past our ego, past our emotions, and when we are aware of and connected to our Divine Mind, we can enter the fourth room of our Soul House—the Astral Room.

The Astral Plane, or fourth dimension as it is commonly known, is like a hard drive for the physical realm. It has a memory of everything that has ever happened on this planet. The Astral Room is home to Spirit—or the illusion of it. It is where we go to look for our deceased loved ones who have moved on. It is the layer of us that mediums connect with. It is where some spirits linger— those who refuse to leave, rather than move on, because they believe they have more work to do on earth. And it is where most of us will bring our awareness when we first venture into the world of spirituality. This room can be a vast and exciting place if you're new to Spirit, and eye-opening when you start to realize what energies are actually housed here.

Let's use this story as an example: A woman is driving down the freeway, on her way to work, and gets a call from her boss, a man she hates. He fires her over the phone. Knowing she is on the brink of losing her home and everything she owns, she yanks the steering wheel on an impulse and hits the white barrier wall next to the fast lane. She crashes and her car flips. She dies on the scene. Ten years later you are driving down the road, thinking about the boss you hate. That similar thought in that place brings you into resonance with the dead woman's experience just enough to have your consciousness gain access to the imprinted memory of her yanking the wheel, crashing, and flipping. Out of nowhere you get a visual of your car crashing into the median next to you and flipping over. Or maybe you think to yourself, *I wonder what would happen if I just turned my wheel and crashed into that wall or another car.* This happens because you are resonating with the spirit of that woman—she has now entered your reality.

I am not sharing this to scare anyone, because honestly it is the furthest thing from scary or creepy when you know what to look for. As you have seen again and again throughout the book, it's all just energy. The trouble is that without your awareness, your brain does not know the difference between your own energy, thoughts, and memories and someone else's.

Using something as simple as the Snow Globe to surround yourself with light and clear out anything that does not belong to you can remedy any situation like the one I described above.

Theta State

Normally we don't consciously recognize energies that don't belong to us when they enter our fields, simply because we're much too busy listening to our loud and active brains. But when we're on a kind of autopilot— when we're doing the dishes, or going for a walk, or driving a familiar route—the brain goes into a theta state.

Have you ever finished your commute and thought, *Sheesh, I don't even remember driving home—that was fast?* This is because your brain took a break, allowing your soul's access to the Astral Plane to take control. This is where we can more readily recognize the energies around us.

Normally the first energies we pick up on are the thoughts other people are having about us. When you suddenly, for no reason at all, remember your best friend from middle school that you haven't talked to in forever? She's probably thinking about you right at that moment.

Theta state is also just a great time to sort through things. When you let yourself wander in this way, you allow yourself to settle unresolved issues and energies. I can spend all day with my husband and we'll just chat about nothing, but if he's been driving for a few hours, he'll call me full of plans for the future, how we are going to pay this and that off and how he was thinking about buying a house and where my daughter will go to school and on and on and on.

This theta state tends to happen to a lot of people while driving, because driving for some is a form of meditation. And often it's a really valuable time. But if you don't make sure you're safe in your Snow Globe before entering a theta state, you won't be protected from energies like those of the woman who crashed her car in the example above.

Grounding Yourself

I know we have already talked a lot about grounding, but now that we're hanging out in the Astral Plane, it is more important than ever. I had a client who had to fly a lot for work, but she was terrified of flying, so she had to take heavy doses of anxiety medication just to make it through. She would be paralyzed by fear from visions of the plane crashing. These weren't necessarily her own thoughts; they were a combination of residual energies and the push of the minds and energies of all the people stuck with her in that tiny flying hallway. With such closeness, so many foreign energies are intertwined and have the ability to penetrate our fields of consciousness.

The simple technique of using a Snow Globe around my client and the plane to clear all that energy has allowed her to eliminate this anxiety and keeps her safe and secure within the bubble of her own consciousness. She no longer has to read the astral imprints of every time the plane has broken down or internalize the fears of everyone else on the plane with her.

As you will hear me say over and over, the brain cannot differentiate between *your* energy, thoughts, and memories and someone else's. The only thing that differentiates your consciousness from the guy next to you on the bus or airplane is the brain that is being used to process the experience.

This is why the Snow Globe, which we learned about in Room Two, is such a powerful and important tool in my teachings. It can be used for just about anything, and it *must* be used to protect yourself from experiencing the darker side of the Astral Plane.

Exercise: Alone in the Snow Globe

Test this statement: "I am alone in my Snow Globe." You can use either your intuition or the muscle-testing or pendulum exercise from Room One.

If you get a yes, great. If not, say, "I am two," and test that. Then, "I am three," and test that . . . keep going until you know how many energies are in your Snow Globe.

Let's say you tested yes for "I am more than 15,000." That means you have the energy of 15,000 people or entities in your Snow Globe, which would make for a very cluttered space and a racing mind because of it. This is not surprising—all of us carry so many energies, particularly in times of crisis, like floods or fires. But that doesn't mean it's good for us. These energies that don't belong to us mess with our thought patterns and cause us to not feel like ourselves, or at the very least they cause us to feel exhausted because they are using our life-force energy.

Once you have determined how many you are, close your eyes and imagine, hundreds of feet above you, a huge bright white Snow Globe with a zero in the middle of it. Allow this enormous Snow Globe to drop into your own Snow Globe. Then test again: "I am one." If you do not get a yes, say with authority, "Source, help me make sure I am alone in my Snow Globe now." Imagine your Snow Globe being cleared in any way you would like and then test again.

Attunement: Quick Snow Globe Clearing

When you go from one place to another, whether it's running errands or visiting with a friend, I want you to notice the energy in the room. Notice how work feels when you are there alone, as opposed to when certain co-workers arrive. Feel how things change, how the energy changes, how the room changes when different people enter. If you notice that your mood changes instantly, at *any* time, just do this attunement to the Snow Globe:

Close your eyes. Say, "I am my I Am."

Take a few deep breaths, imagine you are in the center of your head, and say, "I am (your name) and I am a Snow Globe now."

Imagine you are the statue in the middle of a Snow Globe, with snowflakes and water swirling all around you.

Feel what it feels like to be in your Snow Globe.

Then say, "I am alone in my Snow Globe."

Imagine a huge ball of bright white or golden light dropping down over you, into your Snow Globe, down through your head, through your body, and out through your feet into the center of the earth, where anyone or anything that is not you will be flushed away from you and transmuted into unconditional love through the energy of the earth and the white light above you.

This can take you 30 minutes if you want to make it a meditation, or you can do it in 20 seconds while walking into the office. The key here is that you are becoming aware of the energy around you and recognizing that you and *only* you are in control of how it affects you. If something or someone has energy around them that makes you feel bad, you can protect yourself and clear yourself regardless of the situation because *you* are the creator of your own reality.

Something More

Once we come to accept the fourth room for what it is, and for what resides within, we can start to understand the abilities we all have as well. The crazy thing is, there was always something more about us. We just have been programmed, for the most part, not to be aware of it, unless we've had an experience where we "saw the light."

That was how it happened for me, anyway. It took a series of seizure-induced car accidents in 2008, combined with the death of my ex-boyfriend, to wake me up to the realization that there is just so much more going on in our existence than rooms one through three. When my ex-boyfriend died, my perspective on life fell apart, into a million tiny pieces. I began to ask questions I had never even thought of before: *Where did he go? He never went to church—did he get a chance to go to heaven? Is heaven real? If he makes it to whatever heaven is, what will he do there? Do we really just sit on clouds with harps for eternity? Because I can't imagine him liking that at all!*

These were questions that ran constantly, over and over, in my head, until I began to go crazy. I think any one of us who has lost someone asks similar questions. This is now the type of person I work with on a daily basis, as they come to me for healings or intuitive counseling sessions. Over the last seven years, through conversations with countless people on the other side, with guides, and with angels, I have learned that human spirits living on the other side still have free will, just like we do on earth. From what I understand, we do *not* get swooped off to judgment day, or anything like that, the second we die. We cross over to "the light" only if we choose to.

Some human spirits stay down in the Astral Plane out of stubbornness, or to fix an issue. Some may even be in denial that they have died. These people who choose to stay risk becoming earthbound spirits, and those are the ones I believe the Bible says to look out for. I run into these angry, anxious, and desperate spirits often, and I help them cross over as often as I can.

But the ones I enjoy talking with are the people who went into the light and are safely on their way to their next exciting journey through eternity. The spirits who have completely crossed over say they sometimes return and stay down here anywhere from a few days to a few years, and then they go back up temporarily or for good, depending on what they want to do. Again, they have free will to do what they want. Some stay down here to help family members or even learn from those loved ones who have similar life lessons on their soul's syllabus. We don't always complete all that we came to experience, so learning from loved ones, or even teaching them, once we have crossed over is something that almost every spirit I have spoken with has done in some way or another. I cannot count the number of times I've met a wonderfully loving human spirit who is down here teaching a family member lessons while learning through that person as well. Know that your grandma, or any individual who never quite got the chance to find her passion and purpose in life, may be one of your temporary spirit teachers, helping you discover and love who you are in the midst of this crazy life that the guides like to call "the human condition."

Because of my traumatic experiences, I was sent on a self-guided mission to develop the abilities I have now. I wanted so badly to discover who I was and why I was here. I wanted to know why, during my accidents, I had out-of-body visions of myself screaming over my human body that I didn't want to be Marisa anymore. I wanted to develop my intuition so I could ask this other version of me why she made me come back to earth.

When we have tragedies, accidents, or out-of-body experiences—times when our physical bodies are broken down—our attention is released to another piece of us, in another room of the Soul House. When we come back to our physical mind and body, we sometimes see these other dimensions of self more clearly, like I did. And if this other version of us happens to imprint itself on our consciousness, we tend to awaken spiritually.

But thankfully, you do not need to go through a traumatic near-death experience to have spiritual abilities. The new shift and awakening of consciousness in the world has proven that now we are *all* open to these amazing gifts—it's just up to you to decide if you want to stay awake or go back to sleep.

Are You My Guide? It's Me, Marisa

With all that energy hanging out in the Astral Plane, it can sometimes be hard to tell if an entity you are connecting with is really your guide! Make sure it is your true guide and not an earthbound spirit playing nasty tricks on you by pretending to be your guide or teacher.

Of course, this happened to me. At one point I had about five or six different female energies pretending to be my Creator Self! Talk about having an identity crisis. Not only was I trying to figure out who I was in the physical world, I was dealing with the same thing in the spiritual world. Don't let imposters fool you like they did me. If you feel a connection, do some muscle testing or pendulum swinging, like we learned in Room One, to make sure this is your true guide.

Even though this book is all about *you* and attuning to the true you, it can get pretty lonely when you begin to feel and understand the meaning of oneness. I really want to make sure that, in addition to meeting your Creator Self, you meet a guide! I usually avoid spirit guides because I was tricked way too many times over the years. It was not until I was able to embody my Creator Self that I realized all the guides are just manifestations of that Creator Self, appearing in ways we can receive them so we can get messages from them. So guides can be very helpful, as long as we practice discernment.

The first of these two exercises is *beyond* silly, but it is one of my favorite things to teach. I absolutely love this exercise because it wasn't until my guides taught it to me that I was able to let go of the expectation that God was going to drop out of the sky someday with all the light from heaven shining down upon him and start talking to me. I really thought that was how all this was supposed to work! When I let go of all expectations, I could finally allow myself to see things, like a sudden memory of a movie playing over my head, as clairvoyant messages.

So without further ado, here is one of my absolute favorite exercises.

Exercise: Talking to Your Hair Dryer

Start off by getting yourself into your heart space and aligning with your zero light line. Say, "I am my I Am."

Choose an item in the room that you want to communicate with. This could be your bed, a chair, a saltshaker, the floor, a hair dryer . . . the point here is to show you that *everything* has consciousness, even inanimate objects, and that they can be communicated with, healed, and used in some way, shape, or form energetically.

Now imagine you are in your elevator and ride up to the very top of your head. When the elevator stops, the doors open to an empty space.

In your mind ask the hair dryer (or whatever you chose) to step forward—*as a person* (I know, I said it was silly; but go with me!): "If my hair dryer were a person, what would it look like? Calling my hair dryer in now, as a person!"

From above the open space, a person will drop down, or appear out of nowhere, and walk toward you.

Now talk to this "person" in your imagination. You can ask what their name is, you can ask what their favorite thing to do is, you can ask how old they are, what they like to eat, how they feel about you . . .

When you are finished communicating with "this person," bring your awareness back to your physical body and ground yourself.

Yes, this sounds like madness, but *it is not*! This exercise is training you to use your imagination to communicate with *anything*, even and including your guides.

Our brains have trouble with the idea of communicating with things that don't normally communicate—like a hair dryer, or like energy. So our minds personify those energies and frequencies in order to be able to communicate with them. I believe that's why we see angels as men or women with wings. I believe it's also why so many of us see our spirit guides, which are really just orbs of light, as men with robes and long white beards.

I learned this a long time ago, when I was getting an MRI. My guides came to me while I was lying in the tube, bored out of my mind. They asked me to call in the elements from the periodic table. After arguing with them for a minute or two about how stupid this was, I finally called in oxygen, carbon, and nitrogen. All of them came in, personified.

When I called in oxygen, I saw a beautiful woman, whose presence was refreshing, with her dress billowing in the wind. Carbon came in like a green LEGO soldier. Nitrogen was a little LEGO soldier as well, but he was colored black.

In confusion, I stopped calling in elements and said, "What the heck?"

Then my guides started talking. And talking. And talking. But the gist of what they said was, "You are not human, and neither are we. You are just *in* a human, so you see everything as a human or humanlike form. That's how the mind works. In order for you to know what type of energy you are communicating with, it must have features you understand or can translate through a feeling you get. If you were to see oxygen in true form, you would know nothing about it, but by seeing a refreshed, light, relaxed woman, you can pull from that the characteristics of oxygen."

From that point forward, I looked at spirit guides, angels, and even my hair dryer in a very different way!

If you can help your consciousness understand that you can communicate with anything, you'll stop looking for a person in flowy robes who will speak to you in a thunderous voice (or whatever your preconception may be—that was just mine). You may even be nicer to your hair dryer. Unfortunately, once you go down this road of communication, it can be really hard to focus, because you never know what might start talking to you. I'm not kidding, I'm warning you!

Now, let's put that hair dryer down and do the second exercise so you can get started talking to one of your guides!

Exercise: Calling in Your Guide

Start by aligning with your heart space and the zero light line. Make sure all is clear in your Snow Globe.

Decide what inanimate object you will talk to and call it in, just like the hair dryer from earlier.

Imagine this object you've chosen walking into the room as a person. What do they look like? What are they wearing? How do they make you feel? Are they nice, mean, rude, polite? Ask them questions and allow yourself to imagine their answers. When you're done, say, "Thank you."

Now that you've established you're ready to talk to *anything*, ask that a guide be called in as a person. See who walks through your door. If you get someone who looks scary, sloppy, or bad in any way, ask them to leave, and call in your *real* guide. Your mind knows how to read energy, so if you feel uncomfortable, that's an important sign that this is not your real guide.

Once someone you're comfortable with has entered, you can create a "preset" to call this guide. You can ask them to put a shape, symbol, object, or number into your mind, or you can imagine them holding one of these things. And once you've imagined this, picture it floating toward you or imagine it in your hand, and pull it into your heart. If you do not feel good or expanded by this, ask them for something different. Once you feel good about this symbol, shape, object, or number, say, "Thank you; it is so." And just sit for a second.

When you're done, ground yourself using the technique you learned at the beginning of the book, open your eyes, and bring your awareness back to the physical world. Write anything and everything about your experience down in your journal, along with anything else that comes to mind.

I know you were just talking to a hair dryer and seeing visions of a guide, but writing, recording, or dictating everything is so important because whatever "hair dryer man" just said to you might be something that opens up your eyes to a much bigger picture! If you felt a positive presence and you know it in your heart, then that *was* a guide. It's just a matter of allowing yourself to interpret it as such.

Uncovering Your Gifts

Here is a list of the gifts you may discover in your Astral Room. In reality, we all have all these gifts, but in each person some will resonate more strongly than others. Usually your strongest gifts are in line with those physical senses you use the most too.

Read through the descriptions of these gifts. What resonates with you?

Psychic. He or she reads second- and fourth-room energies around a person, which also includes their lower mind in the first and third rooms. Psychics will sometimes read the person's worst fear, or the thing they are hoping the psychic will not pick up on, because they are thinking about it so much.

Medium. All mediums are psychic, but not all psychics are mediums. A medium by definition is someone who proves life after death by bringing messages from the deceased through from the spirit plane. The issue with many "mediums" is that they are not in fact mediums— they are psychics, and they are reading the field and the mind of the person, rather than communicating with the other side, which would technically be outside of the Soul House.

The "Determining Truth" discernment exercise you learned at the beginning of the book would be a good one to use if you are getting a reading and want to make sure the spirit you are trying to reach is really the one giving you messages, rather than memories from your third room or thoughts from your first room being transmitted through your energy field. A legitimate medium will connect with the Creator Self of the deceased and from there will be able to give messages free of emotional influence.

Unfortunately, there is a limited amount of mediumship teaching due to mediums keeping their secret sauce to themselves. So I will attempt to give you a little helpful insight here. Before they understand the realms they are reading and opening up their clients to, mediums tend to communicate with earthbound spirits that are stuck down here due to second-room emotions they have not processed yet. It is not until they feel better and have closure that these stubborn people cross over. When they feel they have resolved their anger, fear, jealousy, or whatever is keeping them here, that is when they will leave and go back to the soul plane. Mediums who are unknowingly working in the lower emotional astral realms will find themselves eating greasy, cheesy foods, especially when with a group of people. This is because these foods are grounding, and they help keep a medium in the Physical

Room so as to not experience, say, the angry spirit that is following their co-worker around in hopes of apologizing for cheating on them 17 years ago. All spirits want is to say their piece, but doing so can cause issues for those of us who are sensitive to realms like depression and anxiety and an array of physical issues. If an earthbound spirit is around a particular person enough, the living human who is sensitive to the second, third, and fourth rooms can begin to have symptoms of the illnesses the deceased human died from, because it is not until a spirit crosses over that we shed the emotional body and get our etheric body healed.

If you suspect you are a medium, use the Snow Globe attunement often, and muscle test to make sure you are the only soul in your Snow Globe. If not, say, "I am my I Am, and I am alone in my Snow Globe," then watch as light pours down over you and washes away anyone other than you.

Conscious Channel. This is someone who can take their awareness into another being and allow that being's thoughts to run through their own mind, to be translated and spoken verbally in the physical world.

Trance Channel. A trance channel can leave their body completely so that another being may step into their field and use their body to speak and communicate with the physical world. This frequently ties in with automatic writing, which is allowing another being to step into our energy and write using our hand. This is a form of mediumship, though traditional, old-school mediums will say that it is only automatic writing if the person's hand moves all by itself; otherwise it is considered to be inspirational writing, when we write what we are hearing or feeling or sensing but it is us moving our own hand, like transcribing a meeting we are sitting in on.

Clairaudience. This is when we hear words, sounds, or music in our mind. Only very rarely is it in someone else's voice; it is almost always in our own mind's voice. Many times someone with this ability thinks they are talking to themselves, when really they are using their ability to read energy around them and convert it into something they can hear in their head. Those with this ability always doubt they are communicating with Spirit or their higher self because they have heard this voice their entire life. They somehow expect communication with frequencies outside themselves to be more exciting. I know this was the case for me when I first started. I wanted lights from heaven shining down, with a booming voice coming from the clouds! And because I was not getting that, I assumed I was not really connecting with anything outside myself.

Clairsentience. Otherwise known as clear feeling, this is sensing another person or spirit's feelings and thoughts as something physical, like chills, goose bumps, heat, or cold. I have clients who can feel pressure on a certain part of their body when they are about to get a message. My dad and my husband also sense energy this way. The first time my dad and I experienced a spirit visitor together was during church in 2011. My dad felt someone run a hand across the top of his head; when this happened, he flinched and looked at me like a deer in headlights. I looked up behind him and saw my Grandpa Joe smiling and waving at me.

This is not the same as being an empath, who feels others' emotions; this is someone getting chills from everything, whether it's someone talking, music, or thoughts in general. My husband has this; on long car drives when we just sit without talking and listen to music, he breaks out in goose bumps when his favorite songs come on and trigger his memories of good times. It's super cute! These feelers love music because music is frequency, and they can feel it.

Clairalience. This is being able to smell odors that don't have any kind of physical source. The most common smells that people detect are perfume from a loved one who has passed, cigarette smoke, and things like rosemary or cedar. I used to notice an awful rotten egg smell when I first started opening up to Spirit and would wear essential oils under my nose so I would not be hit with the terrible smell. I begged Source to take that ability away, and before I knew it, it was gone. Thank God!

Clairgustance. Like clairalience, this is the ability to *taste* something that isn't actually there. I have never met anyone with this gift, although my old teacher said his grandmother had this sense and could taste cookies when *her* grandmother was around.

Claircognizance. This is when we have knowledge about things we would normally not know. This is the hardest ability for people to recognize or admit they have because it is usually coupled with humongous self-doubt.

Channel. Imagine this: You are getting a coffee at the local coffee shop. Even though you are late for work, this does not stop you from walking up to a lady to compliment her on her watch because she seems sad. You get to talking, and 20 minutes later, she is thanking you up and down for the amazing advice you just gave her as you are running out the door to get to work, scolding yourself for losing track of time yet again! You are a channel, and your Creator Self and her Creator Self are working together to get a message into the physical plane, because she is so blocked she cannot receive it herself. Here's another scenario: you're in the process of writing a highly emotional e-mail to someone, and the next thing you know, it is 30 minutes later and you have written the most eloquent e-mail ever, explaining exactly how you feel. You have just channeled a guide unknowingly.

Healer. Healers are people who have come to this planet to act as conduits for source energy. What this means is that their frequency is higher than the average person's, and even when they are around a lot of negativity they are naturally able to keep their frequency in a place where others feel good around them. Healers are those people who make others feel happy, even if they are not in a super good mood. The downside to being a healer is that you tend to feel pain around others that may or may not mirror their physical issues. If you do not know you are a healer, you are liable to think that you are actually injured or that you have an ailment. You get really hot and cold at random times throughout the day when everyone else seems fine, because you are picking up on and balancing everyone's frequency around you without knowing it.

What Is Channeling?

Because channeling is one of my most profound gifts, I'm going to focus on that a little more. For me, it's a connection with Source that results from a transfer of information, from receiving vibrations from outside my brain. Those vibrations form sentences, delivering messages for me and for others.

As described briefly above, there are two kinds of channels: conscious and unconscious (also known as trance channels). Conscious channels are awake and aware of what is going on and being said. Trance channels have no idea what is going on—they are being animated, speaking with a voice that is not their own. They may speak a language that is not their own too, and their messages are much more direct and powerful because their consciousness is not standing in the way of the connection with Source.

Conscious channeling is limited by our own minds, knowledge, and belief systems, however much clearing we try to do. All mediums and channels have blocks, no matter how evolved or spiritual we claim to be—it is, again, the human condition. Even such simple beliefs as "I don't speak Spanish" will prevent a Spanish message from flowing through, while an unconscious channel will simply start translating the message, without any idea they are doing so.

I am familiar with both types of channeling, but these days I try to achieve something between the two, moving back and forth between consciousness and unconsciousness. Conscious channeling requires much less energy—in fact, it leaves me feeling rejuvenated—whereas trance channeling leaves me feeling groggy and tired.

If I am asking or being asked a question that I have strong beliefs about, or that is about a particularly emotional topic, I know I need to trance channel—otherwise, I'll bring too much to the table myself, and the answer won't be pure and true. It's exhausting, but it's worth it to get to the truth.

This is all a bit black and white, as channeling can get way more complicated, but I just want to provide you with a simple overview. The easiest explanation is that, when I'm channeling, I stand aside and let Source speak through me. That might be an easy explanation, but that's not to say it is easy to do! It has taken years of channeling for hours every day to refine the energies I tune in to. So many channels out there are accidentally (or maybe not so accidentally) channeling things other than Source—those who have passed, claiming to be guides; dark force entities; fake guides; elementals—so we need to be careful.

As always, it's a matter of staying grounded, aligned with the zero light line and your heart space. Trance channeling can be hard to achieve because we block ourselves from it, but *anyone* can be a conscious channel.

Leaving Room Four

We are already higher than most people ever go—but wait, there's more!

The Astral Plane is, as we've discussed, actually a pretty messy place, with a lot of different energies hanging around, sometimes causing trouble. When we step back into the hallway, we will find a purer, less crowded connection with Source.

5

THE GOD ROOM

As exciting as it is to open up to Spirit in the Astral Plane, it's even more exciting when you find yourself in Room Five. Because once you enter the God Room, you can start to really see and understand your life's plan.

From this room comes the divine spark you have inside you, the compassionate witness, the eyes of God who is experiencing all its creations. Feeling the divine spark inside ourselves is so amazing. When I go into this room, I can access Christ Consciousness, which transmits as compassion and forgiveness.

Your Soul House is in the center of your brain, so God really is inside you. If you bring your awareness into this room, you can do *anything* with that unconditional love. You could ask the soul of someone you just *cannot* forgive to come with you, and the light from this room will saturate each of you, healing all your layers. What better place to bring a relationship in need of healing than to the Throne of God?

Some of us might have some issues with the idea of God because of all that is wrapped up in it. Let's try to take away all that baggage and see what's underneath.

God is not a person. I think if everyone understood that, we would have a lot less trouble with this whole *God* concept. God is energy.

In order for us to connect with God, we need to be able to feel God, to feel the aspect all of us have inside that is God. It's like with electricity—everybody believes in that, right? Would anyone ever see a light and say, "Oh, nope, electricity doesn't exist"? Even if we didn't know what electricity was exactly, we would still see that it was there and wonder where it came from.

The other night I asked my mom and my husband to find the spark of God within them. My husband, being a firearms instructor and a precision shooter, said it was in his trigger finger. I thought he was kidding, but he said, "No, I can actually see a spark flying off my finger!" He had just come home from shooting practice, and that was where his awareness was. So it really can be *anywhere*.

Finding that connection with God isn't easy. It is so difficult because we have been given amnesia, because there's so much in the way, because we're naturally skeptical . . . for so, so many reasons. But we do have some help.

We talked a bit about helpful spirits and teachers in Room Four. The best of those, the most powerful and wisest of our guides, can move to Room Five, maintaining their own connection with God, and help us find our way.

Exercise: Finding Your Divine Spark

This is an exercise that will help you find that spark within yourself, that piece of the Divine.

To feel God within you, just stop for a moment. Bring your awareness into your physical body, into the center of your brain, into your pineal gland, and breathe in and out a few times. Remember that God is inside your physical body.

Say, "I am my I Am." Align with the zero light line and your heart space.

Tell your brain to take your thoughts to where God resides inside you. It might be anywhere—in your foot, your abdomen, your heart space, your brain—everyone has their own place, their own direct, physical connection with the electricity that is God. Say, "Show me where my Divine Spark is." Allow your awareness to go there.

Say, "I am now in the center of my Divine Spark. Show me what it feels like."

Wherever you find God, once your awareness is there, sit for a minute or two and focus on this area, allowing your awareness to expand. Visualize the spark as a bright light burning inside you. Let it burn and grow into a bubble that reaches beyond your body. You are taking your highest frequency point and expanding it out through all the different rooms of your Soul House.

You will feel a shift. This shift, this moment of change, is impossible to miss. How you interpret it, though, depends on how open you are, how aware you are. Your mind might start to say, "Hey, maybe there is something out there. Maybe I am connecting with something, but what is it? Is it energy? Is it a person? Is it a thing?"

Sit and allow this feeling to heal you, or ask this Divine Spark to go to a place in your body that needs healing.

The God Spot

My guides have explained that somewhere along the tube of light around our spine that we talked about in the very beginning, we have our God Spot. According to the guides, in our very first incarnation, the God Spot is located at the base of our spine, at our first energy center. Eventually it works its way up to the crown of our head. When the God Spot has ascended to the crown, we are done—we are "Christed," we have graduated from soul school! Being Christed, becoming a creator of realities that souls live within, supposedly takes thousands of lifetimes, and until then the God Spot is the container for our life experience, recording everything we do throughout our lifetime. Within the God Spot, we find the energy varying between the three layers of God: our I Am awareness, Divine electricity, and the personality of God. As we move through the rest of the Soul House, we will get to know the Divine electricity in Room Six and the I Am awareness in Room Seven.

By bringing your awareness into the center of your God Spot, you can experience the glory of the electricity, the light of awareness, and the consciousness or mind of God. When the guides say, "God is within us," they are not joking around, and the exercises that follow to align your I Am with your God Spot will prove it to you.

The guides say that the majority of souls incarnated on earth are what they call level five souls, with their God Spot near their throat chakra. However, it seems that many people, even those with rigorous spiritual practices, have their "thought spot" in a completely different space, down below the hips, in the root chakra! Imagine the thought spot as a bubble of awareness controlled by our human consciousness's level rather than by our soul's level. This thought spot moves up and down with every thought we think. When we can begin to merge the thought spot of our human awareness with the God Spot of our Creator Self and beyond, our lives just get better. It's impossible to put into words what I have experienced through merging my thought spot and God Spot; you just need to experience it the way I, and so many students and clients, have.

According to the guides, our God Spot can be below where it is supposed to be due to our thought spot hanging out in the lower levels too much. This means the soul's consciousness "fell." And if you don't know to check where your God Spot is, you might end up staying there. But I've got a solution!

Reasons for our God Spot ending up in the first energy center, or root chakra, would be:

1. Doing a healing or reading on someone who was existing at the root chakra, or otherwise connecting to them on an energetic level, beyond the physical, and therefore getting pulled down.

2. Having a guide who is not really a guide. (The "Determining Truth" discernment exercise from the beginning of the book will teach you to avoid this happening ever again!)

3. Allowing anger or fear to take control of our lives.

4. Being intimate with someone who was existing in the first energy center. I have had a stream of clients who have gone back to their spiritual practices of taking hallucinogens and having sex with strangers, and have fallen right back down to level one. They feel these experiences get them closer to Source. When they ask if this is the case, I say yes, but not the real Source. If you are involved in these spiritual practices, my suggestion is to use the discernment exercise to see if your heart really agrees with you using this as your way to connect to an unconditionally loving Source—or if instead you should do this God Spot exercise and take your life and your energy back for good!

5. At some point in our lives deciding to hate God or deeming God not real. All my intellectual spiritual friends are in the root chakra; when we do the God Spot exercise together, they always have amazing experiences, and their lives change drastically if they allow it.

When I learned about all this, I was dying to know where my God Spot was located. I asked the guides to lead me through a channeled meditation. When I asked where my God Spot was, I was led to about six feet to my right. I realized that since I was channeling and was technically not in my physical body, I was seeing my God Spot outside me. Right then and there I was able to determine that the God Spot follows the awareness and the light body, not the physical body.

So I pulled my awareness back into my body and asked, "Where is my thought spot?" It was in the bottom of the solar plexus. Then I asked, "Where is my God Spot?" My attention was taken immediately to my third eye.

The guides explained that my God Spot resides at the third eye because I am technically a level six soul, but due to my choices in life, I am *way* behind the learning curve and operating as a level three soul, down in the third energy center, or solar plexus. Keep in mind that this is after massive amounts of self-help work, daily brutally honest mirror work, self-healing, and cord cutting. I was almost afraid to ask where I had been residing when I first started on my spiritual path, because I knew I must have been down in the lower part of the first level.

I was correct. Prior to my accident and eye-opening experience, I was living my life surrounded by the energies and emotions that coincide with the middle of the first energy center. My past suddenly made so much sense! Of course I had been at a lower level, and of course my actions fed that! Rather than being upset at myself, I felt so much compassion for little Marisa, the confused 17-year-old who had decided that since the boy she loved didn't love her back, she hated God for dealing her such an awful life. This compassion has now given even more power to the flame that lights my passion to help young people that age, or even the inner children that age within us, to offer education and teach the ability to connect with and stay connected to their God Spot and their soul's mission, which will give them the life they desire and deserve.

The guides then led me through an attunement process that will allow the thought spot to be taken up one level from where it currently resides. After doing this attunement and pulling my awareness back into my heart,

I could feel a difference immediately. The things I worried about on a daily basis were meaningless. It was amazing! As the days passed, my thought spot would move back down to the same place in the lower solar plexus, but each time I bring it up, it stays in this higher position longer. I can really feel a difference in how I am seeing life, and I have so much more energy.

Here it is broken down into several simple steps, so you can bring your thought spot up to where your God Spot is, bringing yourself to whichever level your soul should be operating at for your highest and best good, in accordance with your soul's purpose and mission.

Exercise: Aligning Your Thought Spot and God Spot

Close your eyes, place your hand on the center of your chest, and begin to relax and breathe. Say, "I am my I Am."

As you relax, imagine a ball of light in the center of your chest. Imagine it expanding while you relax and breathe.

Say, "Zero," and feel yourself sink into the ball of light in the center of your chest. Continue to breathe.

Say, "Zero, ground," and imagine a bolt of light shooting out of the ball and into the center of the earth, securely attaching you to loving earth energy.

Say, "Zero, Source," and imagine a bolt of light securing you to the Source of all that is.

Now that you are attached to the real Source of all, attached to the earth, and aligned with the zero light line, just feel what you feel like and say in your mind, "Take me to my thought spot." You will feel your attention move to another space on your body. Do not judge; just allow yourself to go wherever your attention goes.

You can write down where your thought spot is right now or just take note mentally.

Say, "Take me to where my God Spot is now," and then just allow your awareness and the thought spot to move. When you feel your thought spot merge with your God Spot, you can open your eyes and bring your awareness back to the physical. If your thought spot will not merge with your God Spot, say, "I am my I Am and I command that my thought spot and God Spot merge as one," then watch or feel them merge.

By moving the thought spot to where it would be if you were not an amnesiac soul bumping your way through life, you will be raising your consciousness level in ways that would take a person who meditates daily and does self-healing and counseling years to accomplish. This does not mean you will stay there, but after a while you will begin to notice when you slip and need to bring your awareness to your God Spot. You will need to raise your thought spot back into alignment with your soul's consciousness (your God Spot). By doing this each time, you will completely change your observation point in life. You will eventually get to a point where you are always in line with your soul's consciousness—and when that happens, your soul may move up a level. This is the process of ascension; it ends with becoming an ascended master and then finally a "Christed" soul being that can then create Creator Selves like you, who will create Soul Houses to put a piece of themselves in, so they can experience life and all the lessons and ups and downs that come with being blindly human once again!

Your Master Teacher

As you learned in Room Four, your guides are essentially versions of yourself that your mind interprets as different beings, giving them human characteristics.

But there is a guide that is an exception, and that is your Master Teacher. The Master Teacher is not a version of you—it is your Creator Self's teacher. This is the guide who helped you plan this life, and I work with mine every day. I love him! I think you will love yours too.

> "The mere fact that you are willing to see the flaws within you, to see who you are, what you are, why you are here, we say unto you this, that we are proud!"
>
> —*Excerpt from Your Master Teacher's Letter*

Attunement: A Letter from Your Master Teacher

If you feel drawn to receiving a message from your Master Teacher, please read on. If you do not feel drawn, skip it for now, and when you feel drawn to it, come back and read it then. This message is infused with *your* Master Teacher's energy, and as you read it, you will most likely feel their connection to you. In this letter I channeled the 12 Master Guides who watch over this life experience.

Be honest with yourself and only read it when you want to—or when you don't necessarily *want* to but feel drawn to it. This pure attunement to your Master Teacher, whether you're a beginner or a seasoned professional, will bring a strong, clear connection between you, and it will diminish any connections you have to energies that may claim to be your one true Master Teacher but are not.

A letter to all readers from their Master Teacher:

As we step into your energy today, dear ones, we bring to you the love of a father, the love of a brother, the love of a friend, the love of a mother, and we say unto you this: Each one of you should be proud. Each one of you should see and understand within that you are the Divine. You are brave, and the mere fact that you are willing to see the flaws within you, to see who you are, what you are, why you are here, cause us to say unto you this: that we are proud!

For many of you have had things in your lives that have caused strife; you planned to have these lives where you have been hurt, where you have been beaten down, where you have been battered, just to continue to get back up, look around, and say, "Why is everyone else's life easier?" The simple answer to this is that they may not be here to help others in the same way you are. They are here for other reasons and this is perfect for them. So understand that everything you have been through has been for a reason.

The breakups, the anger, the family difficulties, the financial issues; all these things have made you stronger. And each of you holding this book in your hands today have people in your lives who you know for certain would not be what you are today had they had your *life. They would not be sane. They may not even be alive. For you are all brave, coming to a planet with so much darkness, so much sadness, so much fear, not remembering who you are, but bravely stepping into human form, knowing you would remember the light inside at some point, knowing you would remember even if it meant having to experience the darkest of darkness to find the light burning within.*

So we applaud each and every one of you and want you to know we expect nothing from you, except that you remember how much we love you and begin to see yourself and everyone around you as an innocent four-year-old child: inquisitive, eager to please, impressionable, and innocent in nature. There is not a human on earth who does something because they think it is bad; they do it because at some time in their impressionable life, they were taught that it was good. Remember this when someone says something that you feel hurt by; remember that we can be called in to bring clarity, to heal you, and to help you see that nothing anyone says is ever about you. It is always about them—and all you say and do is about you. This is the design; this is divinity in action. We are all here to experience life in a way that we saw fit prior to allowing our awareness to delve into the density of humanness.

Within your human mind is your subconscious. Look at your subconscious as a room. You are sitting in the middle of it with a walkie-talkie that leads directly to wherever we are. This is the easiest place to communicate from. We will teach you to use this walkie-talkie; we will teach you to quiet the mind in ways that are easy for you in your busy lives. For the hardest thing is to get a healer to heal themselves. Healers are givers, and if you have made it to this portion of the message, you are a healer. Be proud and know that the only way to heal others is to learn to heal thyself first. Love thyself first; then you may truly love another.

Please stay strong; try not to worry. For as you understand more, you will bring even more knowledge in. Having less is scary. You will be ready to manifest all that you've ever wanted to have and all that you've wanted to be. You will even discover new ways to want to be. We promise you this.

We bless each and every one of you; we release all from any false ascension matrix, any religious matrix, that is no longer serving you. We release all from any vows, commitments, pacts, initiations, in past, present, and future lives. We release these from the soul within each of you, in addition to any other aspects of self that accepts healing. We release you now from all energies that are counter to the one true light, the white light of the zero point. You are now free; you have the ability now to choose; you have the ability to decide; you are no longer trapped; you are no longer in fear.

Just feel what it feels like to be free, what it feels like to not have these boundaries while still having the safety. You will feel this shift; you will feel this change. Please understand that you are never alone. Don't wait until you're scared. Don't wait until things are bad. Ask, just ask. The more you ask, the closer we get. Ask us to help with the dishes. Ask us to help you wash the car. The more you ask, the more our energy will connect and the stronger our connection will become. We need to keep the lines of communication open.

We are here with you and we love you. We bless you, dear ones.

Leaving Room Five

I talk to my guides every day, and I love and value every one of them. I don't know what I would do without them. And yet they are not the highest level of *me*. They are powerful, but they are not a direct connection to Source, which is all that our souls long for.

Room Six is not that direct connection either, but it is an essential step to getting there. Your guides have always been, and will always be, with you on this journey. Take their hands, walk back into the long hallway, and open one more door.

6

THE MATRIX ROOM

Hanging out in the God Room can be addicting. It's amazing to start getting the answers to questions that have always plagued you. But sometimes we want answers to things that we haven't necessarily asked for. Sometimes we want to know things like, "When will it get better?" It is in this room that the human becomes inherently aware of *all* the levels of consciousness and how operating from all of them creates a sense of harmony in the world. It is a room of acceptance. Not the *need for acceptance* as experienced in the third dimension, but the ability to accept all the levels of consciousness working together to create a harmonic state.

We've talked again and again about the zero light line, and the zero point. That zero we keep going back to lives here in Room Six. This room is pure energy. Here our minds no longer need to personify that energy, no longer need to differentiate or categorize ourselves. We are not all one, but we are all the zero state, that which exists between the positive and the negative, everything and nothing all at once. And we vibrate, we resonate, in harmony.

This chapter will be on the short side. After all, we have used our connection to the zero point—the zero light line—throughout the book. And, of course, the trouble with a room where you experience everything and nothing is that it's really hard to talk about. But I'll do my best!

The zero point is the matrix of the all-that-is in this created reality. Within the zero point, you can find sacred geometry, echoed on earth in the Fibonacci sequence, in pi, in the golden ratio. You can find sounds, colors, the tints of the universe. The zero point is color, it is number, it is sound, it is form, it is creation—and it is a microscopic version of creation. Any experiences the soul has had, whether on earth in a present or past life or in another life on Jupiter, can be found here. The zero point allows us to feel and experience anything and everything in its true form. We can feel what happiness feels like, feel what joy feels like, feel what abundance feels like, feel what manifestation feels like, feel what anger feels like, feel what knowing your soul mate feels like.

We can bring in the true frequency of anything. We can say, "What does red feel like? What does orange feel like? What does green feel like?" All these different frequencies are programmed and placed within this sixth room—*everything* is here. Your guides who have followed you here will no longer look or sound the same; they may have lost their names. They have become pure energy. But here in this room, you do not need words or images or personifications to communicate. You understand everything and nothing.

Once we realize that everything is made of energy, of frequencies, we realize that we have access to *all* of it. Access to love or greed or anger or fear or jealousy or happiness or joy or peace. All these are frequencies, just the same way as an A on a piano is a frequency. This is what your Creator Self, that piece of God that broke off and came to live in you, uses to program your consciousness; it gives each soul its individuality. I call this the Divine Blueprint. The soul passes through a prism, breaking into different colors, different characteristics, different archetypes. Everything that makes up your I Am is here.

Knowing and understanding your Divine Blueprint can help you know your purpose in life—the lessons that you came here to learn and experience.

Exercise: Zero Point

Say, "I am my I Am." Close your eyes and imagine a tube of light coming from Source down into your head, through your body, and into the earth. Align yourself with the zero light line, as we have done from the very beginning of the book.

You have now grounded your awareness into your body, aligned yourself with all layers of your mind, body, and soul, and you are connected to Source and experiencing life from the zero point. Say, "I am my I Am," and place your hand on your heart. Say, "Zero."

Sink into the ball of light in your heart space. Say, "Zero, ground. Zero, Source."

From above, in the zero point, a huge zero with white light illuminating it will appear. From down in the earth, the same huge zero will appear.

Allow the zeros to move toward you as you continue to sit in your heart space. When the zeros merge, a bright white line will appear in your heart and will start to grow until it connects to the earth and to Source.

When you do this, any snowflakes in your Snow Globe will clear instantly. This is the zero point. You are the zero point.

Source Code Zero

Sometimes we wish we had been programmed a little differently. Maybe we wish that we were braver, that we'd been given a little more red when we went through the prism. Maybe we wish that we were more spiritual, that we had a little more purple.

When we have access to the zero point, we can give ourselves whatever we feel we need. We have access to the source codes. This is literally like the movie *The Matrix*—we can download whatever we want.

Exercise: Source Code Zero

Sit or stand in a comfortable position—do not lie down.

Think of something in your life you would like to change. You may want to write this down in your journal because as you shift things from this level, even if they were huge issues, you will forget they ever existed. It's really quite amazing!

Bring your awareness to your heart space and take a few relaxing breaths.

Say, "I am my I Am."

Say, "Zero," and feel yourself begin to drop into the center of your heart, aligning with the zero light line.

Say, "Zero, ground," and imagine a bolt of light shooting directly out of the heart into the center of the earth and locking you in, like a huge grounding wire stapling you to the earth.

Say, "Zero, Source of all light," and imagine a bolt of light shooting directly up into Source above you and locking you in, the same way you locked into earth.

Bring your attention to the Source of all light and imagine a huge brilliant zero made of white light spinning around above you and say, "Source code zero."

The zero will start spinning so fast it becomes a white blur of energy, quickly dropping down from above you, going through your entire body, through your feet, into the center of the earth, and then back up through you to its original position, sort of like a boomerang.

Say, "I am my I Am," and take as much time as you need to feel like you are expanded into your true essence.

Say, "Divine Blueprint, zero," and watch as the zero does the same thing, this time clearing your entire multidimensional self rather than just your human self, and bringing in any information or healing, using your Divine Blueprint.

It might take a bit of time for the source code zero to complete the task you have assigned it. You may feel a shift over the next few days. It might look like thirst or funky cravings (your body looking to ground itself after such a spiritual experience), or it may be a lack of hunger, as your body floats freely (in which case I would recommend doing some grounding). One thing is certain—you will not feel quite real. You may experience déjà vu or feelings of otherness, or shifts in awareness.

You may have achieved any number of things, depending on what issue you wrote down, including upgrading your inner child to their highest possible expression, returning any fragmented pieces of self to your whole, removing any spirits or intruders and any roots they may have grown within you, and cutting any cords to those who are pulling you out of alignment with your Divine Blueprint (though these may continue to grow back until you uncover what belief is causing them to connect to you).

Your heart will begin healing from the moment you choose to connect with the zero point. From now on, you will go through your life picking up lost pieces and repairing any loss, sadness, hurt, and anxiety. You will need your defenses less and less—eventually leaving no vulnerabilities to protect.

Exercise: Experiencing the Matrix

I have been trying, but honestly there is no way to explain this room. I am going to let you experience it instead.

Close your eyes and breathe.

Say, "I am my I Am and awareness now."

Say, "Heart space, zero." This will instantly bring you into the center of your heart space.

Say, "I am now in my sixth room."

What do you feel like? What do you look like?

Now, because you are in pure frequency, ask to experience the pure frequency of anything, from a feeling to an experience. Be creative!

When you are done, bring your awareness back to your physical body. Feel the room or space around you, wiggle your fingers and toes, and then open your eyes. Make sure to write down anything you experienced in your journal, so that you can refer back to it later. If you do not write it down, you will likely forget it, the same way a dream is forgotten the moment you wake in the morning.

Ground yourself, then go about your day.

Leaving Room Six

I told you the Matrix Room was hard to explain! But it is an incredible gift to be able to experience that level of pure energy. And this room is a portal we must pass through to reach our final, perfect connection to Source— the Creation Room.

> "Many times when the angel of the Lord is spoken of, it is not an angel at all. It is the higher self of that which is the person."
>
> —*The Bible Speaks, Book III: Conversations with Luke and Paul*

7

THE CREATION ROOM

The Creation Room is empty. It is a pure white, blank room. It is a canvas, waiting for you to paint it.

The part of you that broke off from God, that came to live this life, your Creator Self, dwells just outside this room. Here is where all the works of your Creator Self come to be. If the zero point is where your Creator Self went to experience, to practice, to draw up your Divine Blueprint, here in this room is where you sit in your personal power, with all the ability to create that entails.

This room is where you can connect directly with Source. You can, in fact, connect with anything or anyone—you can do *anything* here.

The I Am Observation Room

In our journey through the Soul House, we have reached the end of the long bright hallway. Before us lies a beautiful golden spiraled staircase that leads up to the Creation Room. At the base of these steps is a foyer.

We have been connecting with the mind of our Creator Self, or our I Am, throughout this book. This has allowed us to become any layer of our multidimensional self, and in this room we get to become what most teachers refer to as our Spirit. It is the perfect, joyful, playful, childlike piece of us that wants only to do good. It wants to dance, it wants to play, it wants to experience life. As with the sixth room, there isn't really much more to say about this room, just that it is the self you can use to come into alignment with Source, because it is Source. Our spirit, in conjunction with our I Am, is God experiencing all of its creations, and you now know how to embody this and create with this piece of you. As you can see from how we have used it throughout the book, it makes *everything* possible. Just spending five minutes a day as my spirit by saying, "I am my I Am", getting into my heart, then saying, "I am now my Spirit" and allowing myself to feel what that feels like has changed my life. This simple exercise literally does in five minutes more than an hour energy healing session does in most cases because I am allowing the highest frequency version of me to sit within my reality and heal me.

This morning, for instance, I woke up a complete stress case. I had a to-do list that was a mile long; I had a screaming 5-week-old baby who couldn't be made happy, no matter what; I had a 20-month-old daughter who, because the baby was upset, wanted my exclusive attention; and I had a husband who was even more stressed than I was by the screaming of the baby. So that both of us would not be stressed out, I sent my husband out to run errands. By doing this at least I would not have to deal with his stress on top of my own. This left me with the kids. It also gave me a little bit of relief and some space to think, and I heard in my head, *I am my I Am*, so

I took the cue from my Creator Self and I stopped. I sat down and closed my eyes, and in the midst of all that madness, I took a few deep breaths in through my nose and out through my mouth. I said, "I am my I Am," and I pulled all my attention and awareness into my heart space. I got in my zero light line and my tube of light, and then I heard, *I am my spirit now!* So with intention, I said, "I am my spirit now" and I instantly saw a brilliant human-shaped white light, like what you see after a camera flash. It dropped down into me, then expanded out like a huge balloon and I could tell that I was now inside of my spirit. I was my spirit! Out of nowhere, I heard, *I am my spirit and I need to dance now!*

Miraculously, at that moment, my son stopped crying and my daughter walked over and started hugging my leg and petting me, the way we taught her to pet our dog. (This is what she does when she's trying to show me love; it's the sweetest thing.) I reached for my phone and I turned on my music app and hit play. You know that song from the musical *Grease*, "You're the One That I Want"? It started playing, and I can't describe the joy I felt in my chest, joy coming from my spirit, from my I Am. I literally felt as if someone inside me was laughing hysterically! The feeling picked me up off the couch. I grabbed my daughter, and we danced the entire song through—and then the song played *again,* so we danced again—just like children! My son remained happy, my daughter was thrilled, and my mood shifted *completely*—and my to-do list didn't seem daunting anymore.

Our I Am knows what we need. Do yourself a favor when you wake up in the morning: Just start off your day by saying, "I am my I Am." Pull all your awareness into your heart and visualize yourself here, in your I Am space.

Feel what it feels like to be here, and then ask, "What do I want to do today?" Write down whatever comes to mind. Or, perhaps even better, ask your I Am what *it* wants or needs. When was the last time you fed your spirit?

Exercise: I Am

The following exercise will allow you to become any aspect of you at any time, in any place. It will also allow you to become yourself in the future so that you can see what's to come for you down the road if you make a certain decision. This allows you to heal something that has either happened or has not happened yet. For instance, when I was teaching this exercise in a class, it alerted me to the fact that I would be pregnant in five months. I did not believe it at the time, but I should have—I could have been a little more prepared!

While seated, close your eyes and take a deep breath, in through your nose and out through your mouth.

First make sure to get into your heart, centering in your zero light line and your tube of light.

Say, "I am my I Am." Feel what it feels like to be in that space.

Say, "I am now me in five years." Feel what that feels like, and then say "Zero" to reset yourself.

Say, "I am now me at the happiest moment in my entire life," and feel what that feels like. Say "Zero" to balance out.

Say, "I am now me after I accomplish my goal to _____." Feel what that feels like.

When you are done with this exercise, bring your awareness back into your physical body. Wiggle your fingers and toes, take a few deep breaths, and say, "I am me again, thank you." Ground yourself in any way you see fit and go about your day.

As you can see, you can use your I Am to visualize and truly experience *anything.* You can command yourself into any space or any time and feel what it feels like from there. And you can do this without worrying about picking up the energy from that space. If you were, say, in your mental or emotional body and you were commanding yourself into a space from five years ago and that happened to be a horrible time, you would pick up all the dark snowflakes from that. Then you would have to clear them, and it would be a whole thing. But if you are your I Am, you are simply unable to pick up nasty energies. Your frequency is so high, so bright, so white that nothing can touch you.

Attunement: Entering the Creation Room

Okay. You are now at the base of the stairs, where this entire journey has led you. At the top of these steps is the center of the Creation Room—which is, in essence, your Creator Self's heart space.

Take a deep breath and climb up those 12 stairs.

Say, "I am my I Am."

Get into your heart space, connect with your zero light line, and pull all your attention and awareness into your tube of light.

Sit for a moment and just allow yourself to feel what you feel like.

Say, "I am now Source awareness." From this space of awareness, you are not attached to duality—you are not attached to a self, much less your human ego or intellectual mind.

From this space say, "I am now in my Creator Self's heart space, which I will now call my Creation Room." Feel what that feels like.

From above you, a white pyramid drops down along your zero light line, going through your body and out into the earth.

You have now entered your Creation Room. In the future, when you want to go back to it, all you must do is align yourself in your heart space; say, "I am my I Am," and then say, "Take me to my Creation Room."

Visualizing the Creation Room

Imagine a white room with nothing else in it but a chair in the middle and a table next to it with a button that says SOURCE.

The wall in front of you could be bare or it could have a projection screen so you can imagine images similar to movies being played. Or it could be a whiteboard you can write on or ask your guides to write on.

There should be a door directly to the right of where this projection screen or whiteboard is. This door leads to Source and is a tool you can use to help spirits cross over or call in loved ones from Spirit.

Directly above you there is a huge spotlight. That spotlight is Source energy.

All along the ceiling are little sprinkler heads that are specifically designed to shoot out light, liquid, shapes, sounds, or frequencies. They will emit whatever is needed in order to accomplish what you are asking of Source.

The key to this room, and to creating from it, is to make sure that it is completely empty (aside from what I have described in it) and *white*. The items we have specifically placed in the room are so subtle that they nearly blend in, so the room looks, feels, and seems clear, clean, and white. If you cannot imagine a clean white room, use your mind to imagine cleaning it. You can push things out the door and allow the sprinklers to wash away or dissolve anything. You can even imagine using a spray bottle of cleaning fluid or sweeping up with a broom. You can do anything that feels right in your mind to clear it.

The fastest way I have found to clean my Creation Room is to ask Source for help. I might push the button that says Source so that a blinding light flashes through the room, leaving it perfectly clear, empty, and white. Remember, you can use Source for anything!

Once you've entered into your empty, white Creation Room, you can ask questions of your guides and have them write their answers on the wall. You can call in loved ones, just to hang out. You can ask for healing. You can meditate. This is the place where you can communicate with *all* the universal energies around you. Manifestation from the Creation Room is so much more effective than from anyplace else, because Source can hear you so much more clearly—the frequencies of your mind do not interfere with your communication here.

Attunement: Aligning with the Creation Room

I've described the Creation Room above, but now I want to attune you to it so that you are sure you are aligned and connected to Source, and that everything in it is perfect.

Tip: Once you have done this attunement, all you need to do is get into your heart space, imagine your shape expanding from your heart, and then say, "I am now in my Creation Room." Or just use your imagination to see yourself there. It's as simple as that!

Say, "I am my I Am. I become aware of my physical body." Scan your body from head to toe, taking notice of any pain or any areas you are drawn to. Breathe light into those areas, and as you breathe out, release everything that does not serve you.

When your body is relaxed, say, "Zero." Your attention will be drawn to your heart center. Imagine that you are electricity. Feel what that feels like.

Say, "Zero, Source," to connect with Source. Your zero light line will appear. Make sure it is straight, and if it is not, will it to straighten. If it does not, say, "I command that Source align my zero light line with my spine and all layers of my body now." Witness the line straightening.

Say, "I am now centered in my Creator Self's tube of light." Watch as the tube forms around you, with the zero light line shooting down the center of this tube.

From above you drops a huge ball of light. As you merge with it, you find yourself in your glass elevator. Feel what this feels like. Look around. Is there anything in the elevator with you? (It's okay if there is.) Use the mirrors inside the door to look at yourself.

Push the button on the wall that says GROUND. The elevator will drop all the way down, and when the doors open, neutral grounding energy will rush in, clearing you and anything that may be in the elevator with you. Unconditional love will rush in too, along with any other healing energies you need, whether you are aware of that need or not.

When this is complete, the elevator doors will close. Looking in the mirror, you will see nothing but yourself and the lights on the buttons, waiting for your command.

Say, "I am (your name)." The elevator will begin to move, and when it arrives at a floor on one of the first three levels, the elevator doors will remain closed. Look in the mirror on the doors.

When the doors finally burst open, energy rushes into your glass elevator, removing anything that is not you, that does not serve you and is not on your path. From above, your Creator Self sends a bubble of brilliant healing light filled with whatever you need right now.

Say, "I am (your name)'s spirit now." Your elevator moves again, but when it stops, the doors again remain closed. Say, "Show me what I look like." Just as before, the doors open, and the void comes rushing in to clear out any dead energies or anything else that does not serve you. Energy from Source comes down to heal you. Look around you. Has the elevator changed? Has your reflection changed?

Say, "Show me what my I Am looks like." As our I Am, we rarely look like our current physical form. We are an accumulation of every life we have ever lived. In some cases, we just look like light. Do not worry if you do not see or feel anything.

The elevator doors open, and once more you are cleansed and scrubbed clean. Once more your Creator Self comes down to help heal you.

This time imagine your Creator Self as a shape. It can be any shape, any color, any size. It drops down into your hands, aligning your soul with your Creator Self.

The elevator again awaits your command. Say, "I am (your name)'s Creator Self." This time, the Creator Self does not drop down from above as an orb of light. Instead, the bubble of light that created you, the God Self, comes in to balance and heal your space.

The elevator again awaits your command. Say, "I am, I am, I am. I am all that I am; I am." With this mantra, your elevator makes its final move along the zero light line, up to the floor where you are *the* I Am—not your individualized consciousness, but that piece of yourself that was part of the whole before you broke off to enjoy your own experience.

Your elevator comes to a stop. When the doors open, you may hear angels singing or the hum of electricity; you may see or hear frequency, or you may notice nothing at all.

From outside, a shape forms around you like a bubble. It shrinks around you and disappears into your heart.

Say, "I am (your name)'s I Am. It is done."

The elevator doors close. You are now attuned. Bring your awareness back to your physical body. In order to return to that connection at any time, bring your awareness into the elevator and call in the shape that represented your Creator Self. Allow it to drop into the elevator. When it does, the elevator will rise as high as it needs to or take you anywhere you want to go.

From this place, you can heal, you can meditate, you can channel, you can communicate with loved ones on the other side, you can muscle test without worrying about interference. In this room you can become purified and renewed. Your consciousness is now a blank slate, ready for *you* to choose what is on it.

From this place, you will become healthier and happier; and any depression will begin to melt away.

Attunement: The Creator Self

Now let's meet that Creator Self!

Imagine a tube of light all around you.

Using your mind, pull all your awareness and energy into this tube of light.

Visualize your pineal gland in the center of your brain. Allow your attention to go to that spot in your body and continue to pull any scattered energy and thoughts into the bubble that is now surrounding your consciousness.

From directly above you, a huge bubble of light that represents the Creator Self will drop down the tube of light.

Allow this bubble to merge into you so that you are inside it.

Now let your bubble drop down into the earth. When you get to the center of the earth, allow the neutral energies of Mother Earth to fill the bubble. As it does this, it will clear you of anything that is not for your highest and best good.

Once the bubble is full, allow it to rise on its own and pass through your entire body and up through your crown to the very top of your tube of light.

When it stops, you will find yourself in the middle of a white room—your Creation Room.

In front of you in your Creation Room, you will see a pane of glass. On the other side of this pane of glass is your Creator Self.

Your Creator Self steps through the glass and comes to sit down and merge with you.

Imagine a shape in your heart space, and say, "I am you, you are me, and I love you." In response your Creator Self will say, "I am you, you are me, and we love you." A beam of light will shine down from above through your head, filling your heart space and the shape you imagined, allowing it to expand out until it's bigger than you.

Once your shape has expanded past you, it will disappear. And now you are attuned!

Attunement: Aligning to Your Creator Self

Like I said, this is all a little out there. I still have trouble keeping it straight in my mind. But what I do know is that your Creator Self is the part of you that is most able to access the highest level of communication with Source. So are you ready for your first attunement to your Creator Self? I'm so excited for you! Let's go!

Close your eyes and relax into your breath as we have done in previous attunements.

Imagine a ball of light in your chest and bring all your attention and awareness to it. You may put your hand on your heart to draw your focus there.

Say, "Zero," to center yourself into this space, and continue breathing consciously.

Say, "I am now connected with Source," and imagine taking three steps backward out of your heart space.

With your eyes still closed, imagine there is a mirror in front of you, and in the mirror is the most perfect version of you. It is the you that is *done*. The you that has finished all the life lessons you have ahead of you. This is your Creator Self.

Say, "I am you and you are me." Allow the image in the mirror to merge with you in any way your mind wants to visualize it.

You are now your Creator Self.

Sit for a moment, and take notice of how you feel. Do you feel bigger or smaller? Do you feel hot or cold? Is your mind moving faster or slower than usual? Are you seeing anything within your mind? Are you hearing any noises or song within your mind? If you do not sense anything, that is okay; there is no one way to do this.

Bring your awareness back to your physical body. Become aware of the room around you. Begin to stretch, and wiggle your fingers and toes; then slowly, when you are ready, open your eyes. Make sure to journal your experience so that you do not forget before you go about your day or night.

Congratulations!

Connecting with Source

Connecting with Source is one of the biggest benchmarks in your spiritual awakening, and it is the basis of this book. I can still remember when it first happened to me.

The first meditation class I ever attended was at a spiritual center in Las Vegas. We chanted mantras for an hour. At the time I couldn't believe I was actually at something like that, but I continued to chant the mantra over and over.

After what seemed like only a few minutes, I imagined a mirror was in front of me, and I could see myself in a white gown, wearing a golden crown on my head. I was about eight feet tall, and I was partially blended into my physical body—that is, I could see "Marisa" in front of me, rocking back and forth, chanting with her eyes closed (so I was no longer entirely in my physical body), but I could still feel the cool air in the room we were meditating in. I could hear and see everyone else in the class chanting too, but when I looked around, I saw that many of them also had crowned versions of themselves standing behind them. Some had creepy beings standing between them and their crowned selves. Some of the people had nothing at all.

At the time, I had just started getting into meditation and I had no idea what Source was. I did not believe in guides or even acknowledge that spirits were real. I thought I was just trying to relieve some stress!

Then, in the center of the room, a huge white horse rose out of the floor. It had a ribbon on it, like it had just won a race. I could hear people in the stands cheering for it as it proudly pranced across the room, though I couldn't see them. The horse looked at me and we locked eyes. Instantly, I flew back into my body and jolted awake, like you sometimes do when you wake quickly out of a dream.

After the meditation was over, I innocently asked the teacher about the white horse I saw. You would have thought I was Mary announcing to the disciples that Christ was resurrected! I was immediately swarmed by people from the meditation class. They were saying things like, "Oh my gosh, you are one of the 2 percent: you are one of the ones the white horse has chosen to bring Christ Consciousness to the planet!"

Let me tell you, I ran out of there *so* fast. I probably had smoke coming out of the back of my car as I peeled away. Those people scared me. I felt like I had been in the middle of a crazy cult with that talk about white horses saving the planet. I wanted *no* part of that craziness.

I didn't understand it at the time, but after eight years of daily meditation, automatic writing, and channeling, I now know that experience was me connecting with Source and being conscious of it for the first time ever. I now know that when I feel like I am no longer in my body, when I don't feel quite "real," I am in direct communication with Source. And now, whenever this feeling creeps up on me, I take full advantage of it!

Attunement: Surrounding Yourself with Source

Close your eyes, and with one hand on your heart, breathe in for two seconds. Hold for two seconds. And release for two seconds.

Now breathe in for three seconds, hold for three seconds, and exhale for three seconds.

Do this relaxation routine until you reach five seconds.

Picture a shining ball of light above your head.

Using your imagination, will that ball of light down into the center of your brain.

Continue to breathe, and let the ball expand until it is bigger than your head.

Now say, "I now ask Source into my life, and I ask that all energy, all emotions, all labels, all diagnoses, all memories and feelings that are not me or that are no longer for my highest and best good be sent away now. I ask that Source send me anything I need in order to get me on my highest and best life path so I can be aligned with my mission now."

Visualize the ball around your head dropping down into your chest area, and when it aligns with the perfect piece of Source that resides in your heart, the ball of light will automatically expand out until it is bigger than you.

Just sit and allow this to happen. Feel what you are feeling without judgment. Notice what you notice without judgment. And when your Source bubble is around you, say, "Thank you."

Don't forget to journal or record what you felt and noticed. Connecting with Source is such a life-changing experience—you'll want to be sure you have notes about it!

Exercise: Manifest like the Creator You Are

Here comes the fun part—learning to put all this information together to finally start making the big changes in your life that you've always wanted to make! With all those messages, all that cleaning and clearing, we've been building to this . . . manifesting like the creator you are! Here is how to do it:

Bring your awareness and your hand to the center of your chest.
Say, "Zero."
Say, "Zero, ground."
Say, "Zero, Source."
Sit and allow yourself to connect to the earth and to Source. Feel yourself sink into your heart space.
When you feel relaxed and centered, imagine taking three steps back into your Creator Self, who is standing right behind you.
When you feel as if you are in that aspect of self, or are able to imagine it, say, "Zero." Go into the heart space of your Creator Self.
In front of you is a pond. It is beautiful, and the surroundings are lovelier than anything you have ever seen or felt.

Bring your awareness to how you feel. Look down at your hands and feet. What do they look like? What do they feel like?

Next to you is a scroll of paper and a pen. Imagine reaching over and pulling both onto your lap. Write down an affirmation or desire that you want to manifest.

Imagine a bubble of light encasing the scroll and taking it off your lap. Allow it to float into the pond and dissolve.

Make sure to watch the scroll dissolve completely. By doing this, you are witnessing the dissolution of all the energetic blocks you have to this manifestation. You are watching your manifestation enter the dense reality of earth.

You may meditate here in this reality as long or as little as you like. When you are done, imagine dropping down into your I Am self, just below you. As your I Am, step forward back into your physical self. This will bring your higher consciousness into this reality with you.

Before returning to your day, make sure to ground yourself by imagining roots growing into the earth from your I Am self, which is now in your body. Allow neutral earth energy to fill your body and your I Am.

The Key to Your Past

Here in the Creation Room, you can access anything— including your past, present, and future.

I can still clearly remember a past-life memory that I first had in second grade, when we were doing a week of study on Egypt. I can recall the smell of the musky Egyptian walls combined with the scents of the classroom I was in when this memory hit. Honestly, I don't remember anything else about being seven years old, so why do I remember that? Is it a memory programmed and stored in my soul from a past life? Or could it be another fragment of God?

The fact is, as we become more open, we start to have memories of our past lives creep in. As babies we are so programmed with beliefs and ideas, memories from our own past lives and even some from others' past lives, that when we are born we can't even begin to process or verbalize what we might be remembering, experiencing, or borrowing from another soul's lifetime; we just learn to accept it early on and store it in our mind as our own. So my Egyptian memory could be of me from another lifetime, or it could be something else. Here in the Creation Room, we have access to *all* pasts, not just our own.

Exercise: Stepping into Your Future

The future can be scary because it is unknown—but is it really? If your soul has already downloaded the plan you made when your Creator Self came down to your physical body, then somewhere inside, you already know everything you need to. You just have to learn how to access this plan, which will help guide you so you know when you are on the right track.

Close your eyes and take a few deep breaths, grounding yourself into earth's energy.

Imagine a root, cord, or tube that extends through your physical body into the earth's center and allow it to pull the earth's energies up into your body, through your hips, your torso, your chest, your arms, and all the way up through the crown of your head.

Call forth your Creator Self, which is 12 feet above your head, and pull it into your head.

Now, off in the distance, imagine a staircase. There are 12 steps leading upward. Walk over to them and climb up all the way, to the tenth, eleventh, twelfth step.

Once you get to the top of the stairs, you'll see a long hallway. Allow it to lead you into the light. In that light you'll see a silhouette of a being. This is your soul in pure form.

As you make your way down the hallway toward your soul, feel its energy pulling you, and allow yourself to merge with it. You may feel a shift; you may feel nothing—it does not matter.

Keep walking forward, and as the hallway ends, you'll see something almost like a diving board.

Now set your intention. Ask yourself, "What would I like to know?" These questions can be about anything: "I would like to know how to lose 20 pounds in the next few months." "I would like to know how to get that job I want." "I would like to know how I can make $10,000 more this month." You can ask anything. You can even ask to just be given a message.

Then, on the count of three, you're going to jump.

Ready?

One, two, three . . .

When you jump, your soul is going to take you into one of your lifetimes. You might be able to see things from this lifetime; you might not. You might feel as if you are imagining pictures, seeing things, or you might feel nothing at all. Sometimes your mind will block you from consciously seeing or knowing anything, but don't worry, you are still picking up all the information you need to know and can ask to recall it later on while journaling or writing with your guides.

Stay with this energy for as long as you'd like. Continue to jump over and over, practicing this technique. Or collect yourself and pull yourself back up into the hallway.

Once you return, walk back down the hallway the way you originally came and go back down the stairs. Bring all of your awareness into your physical body, ground yourself, or say something like, "I am now in my physical body and I am grounded." Open your eyes. Don't forget to journal about the things that you saw, felt, heard, or sensed while you were doing this exercise before you go about your day or night.

Remember, in order to do this exercise, you must make sure that your awareness is with your Creator Self, giving you access to the records of your past, present, and future. And you have to give them your permission to share these records with you.

The amazing thing is that once you have mastered this technique, positive shifts will occur in your life without you even realizing it. You can just say, "Take me somewhere that will bring back information that will bring more joy into my life." And it will happen.

Exercise: Source on Speed Dial

Now you have met your Creator Self, you've become attuned to your Creator Self, you understand where your Creator Self comes from, and have connected with Source. But how do you connect to your Creator Self quickly, to get in touch with Source, to make sure you are living life and making decisions that align with your highest good? The fact is, now that you've made it this far, you can *always* get to your Creation Room, whenever you want. It's simple!

I do this next exercise often, especially when I feel like I'm stuck in a rut or I'm starting to get bored with my spiritual practice, with work, or with life in general. I even suggest using this exercise to ask Source to spice up your life! Spirituality can be *fun*!

Go into your Creation Room.

Now, from your Creation Room, ask your Creator Self to call forth any blocks, beliefs, implants, or energies that you may have, whether they are known or unknown. These can be from this lifetime or another one.

Ask these energies to be transmuted with the light of Source so that you may continue on your spiritual path in joy and harmony.

Now watch as energy is brought in to represent what you are calling forth.

Hit the Source button on the table next to you in your Creation Room, and watch these energies all dissolve.

You can now ask that Source pour into all layers of you the virtues, lessons, beliefs, or energies required for you to feel the joy and excitement that you should be feeling as a soul living this amazing human experience.

Watch or feel what happens.

When you are ready, you will come back to your physical reality. You should definitely take note of anything and everything in your recordings or journal!

It Never Stops

The amazing thing is that once you allow yourself to feel all the different layers of yourself and connect to Source, the possibilities are endless.

Once I was able to connect, I realized that our communication never stops—*ever*! I shower, and my mind rambles on with questions; I drive, and the guides or my Creator Self hang with me in the car; I have dinner with my family, and all I can think of are the layers of Spirit. Opening up to this amazing world provides you with constant companionship, support, and excitement, whether you're asking for it or not. It also provides you with the ability to control this human existence of yours in a world that can sometimes seem out of control.

I can't wait to show you how to take all these exercises and attunements you've learned and apply them to everyday life scenarios. But before I do that, there's one more exercise I'd like to introduce you to. This exercise will take into account the totality of the seven-room Soul House that we've been exploring and allow us to finally take charge of it all.

Exercise: Seven-Room Cleanup

We have finally come to the end of our Soul House tour. Before you dive into the practical applications of all this, going forth into the world with all the amazing new capabilities you now know how to use, let's make sure all your rooms are in order.

Connect to your Creator Self and ask that all the energies, emotions, and memories from Rooms One through

Seven that are not organic to your soul's plan, or that are no longer serving your highest and best good, be removed from your Soul House completely and sent back to the light of all creation to be transmuted permanently. Say, "Thank you."

Now go into your Creation Room.

Imagine a small version of your Soul House, with the same seven rooms. See it clearly. Are the rooms different colors?

Then say, "Creator Self, show me what needs to be removed from my third room now" (or whatever room first comes to your mind).

Imagine the Soul House shift in any way your imagination wants to shift it. There may be clouds or goop in some of the rooms. Do not judge, just notice what your imagination shows you.

From above the miniature Soul House, imagine a brilliant light from Source. Its transparent brilliance will come down, and the moment it touches the house, it will immediately be made perfect. All energies that no longer serve you will be released, and all the things you have been holding on to for others will be sent back to Source.

Say, "Thank you," and then repeat with all the rooms or any other room you would like.

I'M PRACTICALLY SPIRITUAL NOW

Now that we understand the different rooms of the Soul House *and* how to access them, we get to take the basics and apply them to our everyday lives! You *can* be spiritual every moment of the day—while driving, as we've discussed, but also while playing with your children, while cleaning the house, while having a difficult conversation with your boss.

You just have to set yourself up for greatness by making time for a little spirituality throughout your day. Taking this time will continue to strengthen your connection to Source and allow you to become a more powerful creator of your own life. Even something as simple as a "soul stroll," as one of my students has named her daily walks, can be an important part of bringing this newfound knowledge into your every day.

The one thing I find most supportive of a spiritual practice happens to be the one thing most of us have difficulty making time to do—meditation. "I don't have time to meditate" is the biggest complaint I hear from my clients and students, and frankly, it's the biggest complaint I hear from myself.

While I was complaining about having no time for myself one day, the guides told me that I was not meditating enough. But how am I supposed to meditate when I have no time for myself? They answered by pretty much bombarding me with a hard look at where my time was spent. And, well, I was a bit embarrassed by what I saw.

So before you start complaining that you don't have time to meditate, become psychic, or learn these techniques and exercises, because life is too demanding, check yourself and your use of electronics. When I stopped spending so much time texting, hanging out on Facebook, BuzzFeed, whatever (you know what I'm talking about), things got so much better. My husband noticed; I became much more attentive to my life, my family, and of course to him. And I realized no one was dying because I didn't respond to their texts, e-mails, or questions immediately. In fact, in most cases people had totally resolved their own issues by the time I got back to them!

Exercise: Take a Soul Bath

Finding the time to meditate and relax is almost impossible in our busy lives, but we all have to bathe or shower every day, so I have come to really look forward to this alone time with my guides and Higher Self. The following is one of my favorite spiritual practices. I call it the Soul Bath! It's such a wonderful gift we can give ourselves.

Schedule a time when you will give your soul a bath. Do not show up late for your appointment.

If you would like, turn on some relaxing music. I suggest putting your phone on airplane mode if you use that to listen to music. Doing so will assure that the energy from someone calling you does not interrupt your Soul Bath. The best thing to do would be to turn off all your electronics. If you must keep them on, leave them outside the bathroom so you will not be tempted to get up and grab them.

Ask your Creator Self what fragrance oils or soaps your soul would like to use today and go with the first thing that comes to your mind if you agree with the choice.

Fill the bathtub and add your fragrances.

Add 1 cup of Epsom salts.

Get into the bathtub and enjoy your bath for at least 20 minutes.

While you are in the bath, begin to breathe in through your nose and out through your mouth, pulling all your awareness and energy into the space around you.

Then say, "I am (your name) now." Bring your awareness into the center of your chest, breathing in through your nose and releasing your breath with a sigh. You will actually feel your heart center vibrating when you do this, and then you can allow your attention to sink deeper into this area.

Say, "Come back." This will call back all the little pieces of your attention that have been scattered throughout the days, weeks, months, or even years. If you are visual, imagine little tendrils of energy being pulled back into your heart; if you are more prone to feeling, feel them come back and make you fuller. If you are a "knower," you'll just know when your attention has come back.

Once you feel centered within your heart, imagine a line—anything from a thin thread to a very thick cord—extending from the bottom of your tub all the way down into the center of the earth. This electrical wire, or grounding wire, will connect your bathwater with the neutral zero point energy in Mother Earth and the frequency it carries.

Imagine there is light shooting up through this cord and filling your bathwater, or imagine that you've plugged into the center of the earth and just leave it at that. (The intention will do it, but I am more of a visual person, so I like to imagine things.)

Now that all your awareness is in your heart, your Creator Self has complete access to your brain, so the thoughts you are thinking (at least 50 percent of them) are coming from your Creator Self.

Ask yourself, "What do I need to wash out of my life?" Think of the things you would like to get rid of in your life, whether they are emotions, thoughts, fears, or people. Imagine all those things as dirt on your body.

Using the water, pretend you are rinsing off the dirt. And as the dirt touches the water, the fragrance, and the salts, transmute it in your imagination and make it disappear.

After you feel you've gotten rid of all these surface things that you're conscious of, take the time to lie back, relax, and do a silent meditation, a guided meditation, or self-healing, or just continue to listen to some music.

When your meditation is over, you may find you have more "dirt" on you that your Creator Self was able to bring to the surface for you to release. So, using the water again, rinse this energetic dirt off of you and imagine it disappearing in the water.

When you are done with this amazing Soul Bath, get out and dry off, but don't let the water out of the tub just yet. Wait to let the water out until you're ready to sit down and, with intention, put any extra energies—known or unknown, seen or unseen—into the water and watch them wash down the drain. By taking the time to do this, you are cleaning out any hidden energies in your aura that you were not consciously aware of.

Once all the water has gone down the drain, plug the drain up and say, "Thank you. It is so, it is so, it is so." Then thank your Creator Self, your soul, and your guides for a job well done with a simple "Thank you."

Exercise: Shower Your Soul

While the Soul Bath is an amazing and healing experience, it is not something that we can always find time for, even with all our efforts to prioritize our spiritual practice. I understand that. My babies definitely don't always let me enjoy a nice soak in the tub! We are all extremely busy and a long drawn-out bath and meditation just isn't in the cards. So I suggest taking a quick shower to heal yourself daily! This is an easy way to clear your energy when you don't have the time for your Soul Bath.

Take a shower as you normally would, pampering yourself as much as you can, using soaps and oils that bring you pleasure. Once you're clean, just stand under the falling water.

Close your eyes and bring all your awareness into your heart center.

Say, "Zero."

Say, "Zero, ground."

Say, "Zero, Source."

Once you feel you are tethered to the heavens and the earth, say, "Show me everything I need to rinse away now."

Imagine that you are Pig-Pen from Charlie Brown, with dust flying around everywhere.

Bring your awareness now to the showerhead and say, "Zero." By doing this all the light from the zero light line you have running through you will reach out and surround the showerhead with zero point energy.

Imagine all the dust washing away and going down the drain.

Once your Pig-Pen mess is clean, imagine a huge version of yourself dropping down directly from above you, shrinking down to your size and entering into your body, aligning its feet with yours, its legs with yours, its arms and head with yours.

Then say, "I am (your name)." This will align you with your I Am self for the rest of the day or night. I usually ask if there's anything else that needs clearing, so that your Creator Self can bring forth anything you may have missed, but it's not always necessary.

Exercise: I Can't Stop Eating!

The more you get comfortable with your newfound abilities, the more changes you will start to see in your life—like the fact that you are constantly eating to keep yourself grounded.

Eating to ground yourself is a practical part of spirituality, but unlike the Soul Bath and the time-making suggestions, eating to ground yourself is not always one of the preferred new practices of a spiritual awakening. It happens because your energy guides are trying to lower your vibration, to protect you from venturing too far from your physical self. This is helpful of them, of course, but it may not be the method of grounding that our physical selves prefer!

When you notice yourself wanting salt or sugar, pastas, or heavy "comfort foods," take a minute and think if this is something you actually want. If so, great! We all love and need a little comfort. But if you're just in need of grounding, do yourself a favor and try another way.

If the weather allows for this, you can go outside barefoot. Stand in the sand or the dirt. Stand in the grass. Just stand outside on the earth. If you live in a colder climate, you can go outside and just pretend that you are barefoot. Either way, visualize the earth being a vacuum. It will vacuum out all the kinetic or fast-moving energies that are causing you to feel ungrounded or "unhinged" (this term is actually referring to the mind becoming disconnected from the body). So go outside, allow all this energy to be released into the earth, and allow the earth's calming energy to flow into your body through your feet. Once you are able to fill your entire body with the healing nature of Mother Earth's energy, you will feel grounded again.

If you want to take this a little bit further, you can ask that any energies that were causing you to need this "comfort food" not only be released from you into the earth, but also be transmuted into unconditional love and sent back to Source.

Now that we've found time, put down the food, and cleared, cleaned, and scrubbed, I'd love to show you a few more practical exercises you can use in everyday situations. These are more specific than the exercises I've shared already, but they are just as important in your daily efforts to remain connected to Source and the path you've discovered for yourself.

Exercise: Help! I Can't Breathe!

This first exercise is for when you feel like you have lost your breath. It's what my mom and I refer to as feeling like "there's a fat man on my chest!" Here's what to do when you have this feeling come upon you:

Find a place where you will not be interrupted for about five minutes, even if it means you have to sneak away to the restroom or your car while you're at work. (Hey, I've done it!)

While standing or sitting with both feet on the floor, legs uncrossed, close your eyes and imagine yourself in your Creation Room.

Say, "I am my I Am." Then say, "Thank you." Some people feel such relief here that they do not need to go on to the next step, but I suggest moving forward unless time is of the essence.

Identify where you feel pressure in your body. Place your right hand there.

Close your eyes and ask to be shown a symbol that will represent this stressor. You may see a shape, a swirling color, a being, or even a word—just roll with whatever you see. (I usually see numbers, and they are always random.)

As soon as a symbol comes into your awareness, ask, "How does it feel?" Does the symbol feel like anxiety, fear, nervousness, anger, sadness? Sometimes you will get something; other times you will be so flipped out that you are blocked. This is okay; go ahead and move on to the next step. Naming the feeling is not pertinent in successfully clearing yourself, though if you can identify the root emotion, you can usually remedy the issue on a much broader scale so eventually the attacks stop happening.

Take a nice cleansing breath in through your nose and out through your mouth, and close your eyes if they're not already closed. Continue to sit or stand in an upright position with both feet securely on the floor.

At your own pace, take one huge breath in through your mouth, hold it for one second, then exhale. Take another breath in through your mouth, filling your lungs comfortably full, hold for two seconds, and then exhale slowly with a sigh. On the third inhale, breathe your awareness into the area that you have your right hand resting on. Bring to mind the symbol you saw, and imagine it underneath your hand, inside your body. Inhale deeply again, as if that area were your lungs and all the air was going into it. Hold this breath as long as it is comfortable without straining—no more than five seconds—and on the exhale, imagine that the symbol comes out of your body with your breath and lands on your Creation Room's white table.

Say, "I am my I Am, and I command that anything on the table, and anything associated with it, seen or unseen, known or unknown, be zeroed out now."

From above the table, imagine another symbol that looks exactly like the one you have on the table dropping down from the roof. When the two touch, they cancel each other out and disappear into thin air, leaving nothing but a huge, glistening, white ball of electricity.

With your mind, will the beautiful ball of pure Source energy into the area you have your hand on. Rather than visualizing this, try to *feel* what it feels like to have pure Source energy filling this part of your body, which was acting as a drama magnet for whatever reason and will continue to do so until you find out what you are trying to accomplish. This ball of Source energy is programmed with the intention to give you what you need on all levels so that you do not need to keep creating the same drama over and over.

Although sometimes doing this exercise just once clears the experience completely, sometimes I have found that it takes a few times to work, so please be patient.

Do Not Discount Your Thoughts

One thing that I have learned over the last six years is that ignoring your thoughts is the last thing that you want to do. When I was learning to meditate I thought that I needed to have an empty mind; I thought that my thoughts were to be ignored so that I could eventually get messages from Spirit. This is the furthest thing from the truth! Our mind is what Spirit uses to communicate with us. Whether it be through dreams, daydreams, visions, or plain old thoughts, the things that continue to come to mind over and over should be looked at as possible messages from the other realms. So do not discount *anything* you see in your mind over and over, even if you are just daydreaming.

The mind is a powerful resource for your spirituality. Awareness of everything that goes on in it is important, but so is *acceptance* of its messages. Nothing that goes on in your mind is by chance. Everything that our attention is brought to means something, though it may not ultimately mean what you think it does now. That is okay, because we are receiving the exact message we need at the exact time we need it, even if we find its meaning has changed for us later.

When you start to see, hear, imagine, or think something over and over, stop and ask yourself the following questions:

1. What does this mean to me now?
2. What did this mean to me 10 years ago?
3. What will this mean to me in 10 years?

By answering those three questions, you will be able to derive a message from anything you experience in your mind.

> "Trust me, I know what I'm doing."
>
> —*The Universe*

CONCLUSION

Maintaining Your Connection

I hope you have enjoyed this journey. It is my express goal to bring everyone into the awareness of their Creator Self and of Source. If I have at least reached one person by sharing these ways to get in touch with the you that is the real *you*, then I know I am fulfilling my life's purpose. Thank you. It has been my honor.

If there is one thing I would like everyone to take away from this book, it is *awareness*. All the different rooms of the Soul House have been accessed through our awareness. It is only when you begin to see life and your I Am through all its different vantage points that you can begin to realize your true connection to Source.

Source is the awareness; the consciousness is the creation.

The awareness witnesses all, and the mind (consciousness) processes it all. The mind never leaves the body, but the awareness does. And when the two merge, when consciousness becomes aware, they bring about the Creator Self.

I want to leave you with a channeled benediction to send you forward with all that you have learned, with all the unconditional love, awareness, protection, grounding, and power that you have. (Note: this channeled information has been edited slightly, but represents the resonance, if not the exact words, of the guides.)

If you feel you have ever disconnected yourself from that which is Source inside you, we would like you to imagine that you are the light that is inside you, a light that is burning bright, a light that will never go out. You can cover it up, you can wrap it in dark paper and smother it in goop, but it will never go out. This light inside you is you *and it is a beacon.*

Feel this light. Say, "I am my Divine Light." Feel what it feels like to be this light. We reignite this light at this time. And we release you from the pain, from the fear, from the regret, from the anger, from that which comes with being human.

And we bring to you a new hope. A new hope and understanding that as you can begin to encourage yourself and believe in yourself, as you can begin to define yourself, you will begin to finally see why you are here. You will see why you want *to be here.*

You are here because you want to enjoy life and the relationships you have in this life. You are here to experience interpersonal relationships, family relationships, and to have fun doing it. You are here to be loved and to love others.

This is it; this is all. Anything else is extra. So what you must do is begin to feel that Divine Light inside you—ask to feel what that feels like—and when you can bring your awareness into that for even two minutes and forty-seven seconds a day, you can see that this alone will heal you. This alone will heal the worries in your life, the pain in your life. This will change your life—forever.

Know that you are that Divine Light, that diamond inside, a diamond that was pressured until it became so bright that it was everlasting and ever-sustaining. You are that diamond, and it resides right above your heart. All you must do is bring yourself into it and become it and allow it to heal your life.

ACKNOWLEDGMENTS

Jeff, thank you for loving me and being so patient and supportive as you've watched me and our life change over the last 10 years. You are my best friend, my rock, and the best husband and father to our children I could have hoped for in life. Thank you for being my hot, hard-core guy. I love you!

Papa, when we became estranged for a year after 14 years of living hell following high school, I was forced to find the me that wanted to live and to love myself in the way I wanted so badly to be loved by others but was not willing to see or allow. You are one of my best friends, my dad, and my spiritual partner in bridging the gap for Christ Consciousness to fill this planet, and I love you for it! Thank you for being you, and thank you for believing in me when I was incapable of believing in myself!

Mama, I could not have written this book without you! Thank you for helping me survive motherhood. You have always encouraged me to be what I am today, even when I thought the things you loved, like yoga or meditation, were crazy. I am so proud you are my mama—even though you want to live in a van!

ABOUT THE
AUTHOR

Marisa Moris is a spiritual intuitive, clairvoyant channel, and quantum Reiki master teacher. She is the creator and founder of Intuition, where she offers readings, healings, and teachings in mediumship, intuition development, meditation, and Christ-centered New Age studies. Intuition is located in sunny Encinitas, CA, where Marisa lives with her family.

Website: www.discoverintuition.com

We hope you enjoyed this Hay House book. If you'd like to receive our online catalog featuring additional information on Hay House books and products, or if you'd like to find out more about the Hay Foundation, please contact:

Hay House, Inc., P.O. Box 5100, Carlsbad, CA 92018-5100
(760) 431-7695 or (800) 654-5126
(760) 431-6948 (fax) or (800) 650-5115 (fax)
www.hayhouse.com® • www.hayfoundation.org

———

Published in Australia by:
Hay House Australia Pty. Ltd., 18/36 Ralph St., Alexandria NSW 2015
Phone: 612-9669-4299 • *Fax:* 612-9669-4144 • www.hayhouse.com.au

Published in the United Kingdom by:
Hay House UK, Ltd., Astley House, 33 Notting Hill Gate, London W11 3JQ
Phone: 44-20-3675-2450 • *Fax:* 44-20-3675-2451 • www.hayhouse.co.uk

Published in India by: Hay House Publishers India,
Muskaan Complex, Plot No. 3, B-2, Vasant Kunj, New Delhi 110 070
Phone: 91-11-4176-1620 • *Fax:* 91-11-4176-1630 • www.hayhouse.co.in

———

Access New Knowledge.
Anytime. Anywhere.

Learn and evolve at your own pace
with the world's leading experts.

www.hayhouseU.com

Hay House Podcasts
Bring Fresh, Free Inspiration Each Week!

Hay House proudly offers a selection of life-changing audio content via our most popular podcasts!

Hay House Meditations Podcast

Features your favorite Hay House authors guiding you through meditations designed to help you relax and rejuvenate. Take their words into your soul and cruise through the week!

Dr. Wayne W. Dyer Podcast

Discover the timeless wisdom of Dr. Wayne W. Dyer, world-renowned spiritual teacher and affectionately known as "the father of motivation." Each week brings some of the best selections from the 10-year span of Dr. Dyer's talk show on HayHouseRadio.com.

Hay House World Summit Podcast

Over 1 million people from 217 countries and territories participate in the massive online event known as the Hay House World Summit. This podcast offers weekly mini-lessons from World Summits past as a taste of what you can hear during the annual event, which occurs each May.

Hay House Radio Podcast

Listen to some of the best moments from HayHouseRadio.com, featuring expert authors such as Dr. Christiane Northrup, Anthony William, Caroline Myss, James Van Praagh, and Doreen Virtue discussing topics such as health, self-healing, motivation, spirituality, positive psychology, and personal development.

Hay House Live Podcast

Enjoy a selection of insightful and inspiring lectures from Hay House Live, an exciting event series that features Hay House authors and leading experts in the fields of alternative health, nutrition, intuitive medicine, success, and more! Feel the electricity of our authors engaging with a live audience, and get motivated to live your best life possible!

Find Hay House podcasts on iTunes, or visit www.HayHouse.com/podcasts for more info.